1993

HERMES BOOKS

John Herington, General Editor

PINDAR

D. S. CARNE-ROSS

YALE UNIVERSITY PRESS
NEW HAVEN AND LONDON

Designed by Sally Harris
and set in Palatino type by
Brevis Press, Bethany, Connecticut.
Printed in the United States of America by
Vail-Ballou Press, Binghamton, New York.

Library of Congress Cataloging in Publication Data

Carne-Ross, D. S.
    Pindar.

    (Hermes books)
    Bibliography: p.
    Includes index.
    1. Pindar—Criticism and interpretation. I. Title.
PA4276.C36 1985   884'.01   84-40668
ISBN 0-300-03383-4
ISBN 0-300-03393-1 (pbk.)

10 9 8 7 6 5 4 3 2 1

FOR TERESA, συνεργῷ

CONTENTS

FOREWORD

"IT WOULD BE A PITY," SAID NIETZSCHE, "IF THE CLASSICS should speak to us less clearly because a million words stood in the way." His forebodings seem now to have been realized. A glance at the increasing girth of successive volumes of the standard journal of classical bibliography, *L'Année Philologique*, since World War II is enough to demonstrate the proliferation of writing on the subject in our time. Unfortunately, the vast majority of the studies listed will prove on inspection to be largely concerned with points of detail and composed by and for academic specialists in the field. Few are addressed to the literate but nonspecialist adult or to that equally important person, the intelligent but uninstructed beginning student; and of those few, very few indeed are the work of scholars of the first rank, equipped for their task not merely with raw classical erudition but also with style, taste, and literary judgment.

It is a strange situation. On one side stand the classical masters of Greece and Rome, those models of concision, elegance, and understanding of the human condition, who composed least of all for narrow technologists, most of all for the Common Reader (and, indeed, the Common Hearer). On the other side stands a sort of industrial complex, processing those masters into an annually growing output of technical articles and monographs. What is lacking, it seems, in our society as well as in our scholarship, is the kind of book that was supplied for earlier generations by such men as Richard Jebb and Gilbert Murray in the intervals of their more technical researches—the kind of book that directed the general reader not to the pyramid of secondary literature piled over the burial places of the classical writers but to the living faces of the writers themselves, as perceived by a scholar-humanist with a deep knowledge of, and love for, his subject. Not only for the sake of the potential student of classics, but also for the sake of the humanities as a whole, within and outside academe, it seems that this gap in classical studies ought to be filled. The Hermes series is a modest attempt to fill it.

We have sought men and women possessed of a rather rare combination of qualities: a love for literature in other languages, extending into modern times; a vision that extends beyond academe to contemporary life itself; and above all an ability to express themselves in clear, lively, and graceful English, without polysyllabic language or parochial jargon. For the aim of the series requires that they should communicate to nonspecialist readers, authoritatively and vividly, their personal sense of why a given classical author's writings have excited people for centuries and why they can continue to do so. Some are classical scholars by profession, some are not; each has lived long with the classics, and especially with the author about whom he or she writes in this series.

The first, middle, and last goal of the Hermes series is to guide the general reader to a dialogue with the classical masters rather than to acquaint him or her with the present state of scholarly research. Thus our volumes contain few or no footnotes; even within the texts, references to secondary literature are kept to a minimum. At the end of each volume, however, is a short bibliography that includes recommended English translations, and selected literary criticism, as well as historical and (when appropriate) biographical studies.

In these ways we hope to let the classics speak again, with a minimum of modern verbiage (as Nietzsche wished), to the widest possible audience of interested people.

John Herington

PREFACE

SINCE THIS BOOK IS ADDRESSED PRIMARILY TO THE GENERAL reader, I have felt bound to assume no knowledge of Greek. I hope of course that there may be something here for those who do have Greek or at least "some" Greek—classical students, comparatists, poets or lovers of poetry brave enough to stumble their way into forbidden linguistic territory, and perhaps some professional Hellenists. I cross swords with a few of them here and there, so they may care to look over my pages to see where I have gone wrong. *Qu'ils soient les bienvenus.*

A word on the shape of this book. It begins with an account of the poetic form in which the bulk of Pindar's surviving work has come down to us, the victory ode. This type of composition is quite unlike anything found in later literature, so rather than go on and devote chapters to this or that broad aspect of the poet's art, I try instead to give some impression of what it "feels like" to read a victory ode, to suggest the way the thing works, how it moves and breathes, by means of a series of rather close readings of individual poems. If I am at all successful, this may do something to free the odes from that marmoreal closure time and learning have imposed upon classical literature, and recover the vital instability which allows a text to reveal different facets of itself and generate new meanings.

To get really close to a poem is possible only if one is

reading it in the original. And yet, no knowledge of Greek being assumed, Pindar appears here in translation (ad hoc affairs of my own making, substantially faithful, I hope, but taking some liberties with the letter—some compound epithets had to be abandoned—in the interests of readable English). How come? Let me admit to a deception I have sought to practice. As I point to features of a line or passage, present only in Pindar's own words, the fiction is that we are *really* meeting him in Greek, the English versions serving merely for the ease of quick consultation. Just beside them, breathing life and fire into their nerveless frames, the great original lies open, luminously. How far this ploy works is for the reader to decide. (He will probably find it helpful to read through an ode once or twice in translation—perhaps the recent one by Frank J. Nisetich—before considering what I have to say about it.) If a single person is provoked into learning enough Greek to tackle Pindar directly, my dearest hope will have been realized.

Only Pindar's epinician or victory odes are treated here. Alexandrian scholarship, when it set about editing his collected work, divided it into seventeen books of which only four, those containing the victory odes, have survived. (These four ancient books fit comfortably into a single modern volume.) Each book is devoted to one of the four great games or festivals, "the games which men call sacred," as Pindar puts it—Olympian, Pythian, Nemean, and Isthmian—and within these books odes are arranged not chronologically but for the most part according to the prestige of the contest involved. (Horse racing, a rich man's pursuit then as now, ranks before boxing or wrestling.) The reader who feels doubtful about how far the versification of athletic events can claim his attention may rest assured: Pindar is not what we mean by a sports correspondent.

Of the other thirteen books we possess numerous fragments, some of considerable length, many of great interest
and beauty. Reluctantly I have said next to nothing about this
material. To have done so would have required discussion of
the different genres Pindar worked in—paians, dithyrambs,
dirges, maiden songs and the like—which would not have
meant much to the reader I have in mind. Nor would it have
served the purpose of this book, which is not to provide information (readily available in the histories and handbooks)
but rather to convey some experience of Pindar's poetry. This,
I judged, could best be done by concentrating on complete
texts. We have forty-five victory odes, quite enough to deal
with in a short introductory study.

Of these odes a dozen have been chosen for detailed
treatment. My choice is I hope representative but it is arbi-
trary to the extent that a quite different selection would have
been possible. I have picked no poem that seems to me dull
or unsuccessful, but on the other hand I have not tried to
single out the "greatest" poems. The first Olympian ode, one
of the most famous, is not here, nor are the seventh Olympian
or third Pythian, among the finest. I have not made a point
of choosing problem poems although at least one such poem,
the seventh Nemean, is included, not because it is problem-
atic but because it is beautiful. What might have been expected, and again is not here, is any attempt to trace Pindar's
poetic development. This would require dates and only about
half the odes can be dated. For the Olympian and Pythian
odes we do have dates, reasonably secure for the most part,
derived from ancient victory lists. No such information is
available for the Nemean and Isthmian odes and we have to
admit that we do not know when most of them were written.
The dates formerly assigned to them and still found in some
editions are based on a biographical, historical reading that

has been largely discredited. For a poet like Pindar this matters less than one might suppose, partly because the epinician genre had its own conventional procedures which the writer was required to observe, more because Pindar found his form early and stuck to it. The earliest datable poem, the tenth Pythian, written in 498 B.C. when the poet was twenty, is already wholly and unmistakably Pindaric.

A chapter on the poet's life and times, this again might have been expected in an introductory study. We have however little solid information about Pindar's life, and since there is a question as to how far his times enter into and affect his work, the matter can I think best be handled in the context of particular poems. The century in which Pindar wrote was intellectually and politically one of the most momentous known to us, yet Thebes, where the poet was born in 518 B.C., stood outside the intellectual movements of the time, and her conduct during its greatest political event—the city sided with Persia when Xerxes invaded Greece in 480—was not something the poet felt called on to celebrate. Traditional, conservative, Thebes was no doubt a provincial place; Pindar, though, spent quite enough time away from Thebes to deprovincialize himself if he so wished. It is reported that as a youth he studied music and poetry in Athens, and his career, as the poet of pan-Hellenic stature he became, led him to many parts of the Greek world. The older view, now questioned, is that he was ignorant of or at least incurious about the New Learning of Ionia and Athens. However, a remark he is credited with—"the students of natural science are plucking the flower of wisdom unripe"—suggests a different attitude, critical rather than ignorant. We may perhaps imagine him saying, with Yeats, "They have schooling of their own, but I pass their schooling by."

The poet's thinking, it is commonly held, was archaic.

This too can be overstated and we are reminded that Pindar was not "an unquestioning transmitter of archaic values." Unquestioning, no, but his values are still archaic in a way and to a degree no longer possible for the great Athenian poets of his time. Sophocles was at heart no less a man of the old covenant and yet he had to face, as Pindar did not, the dissolution of many traditional beliefs and usages. Where Sophocles can declare, through the mouth of the aged Oedipus, "Slow are the gods to mark but they mark well the man who sets divinity aside and turns to madness," Pindar can announce simply, "It becomes a man to say beautiful things of the gods."

Thanks to the archaic cast of his thought, it has often been said, Pindar has no sense of history. Writing for communities involved in political upheavals and for athletic victors themselves sometimes actors on the historical stage, he dissolves politics and history into the timeless form of myth (heroic legend or saga would often be more accurate terms). Perhaps we may get at this matter, which is important since it affects the way we read the odes, with the help of Lévi-Strauss's concept of "mythical history" which "presents the paradox of being both disjoined from and conjoined with the present. It is disjoined from it because the original ancestors were of a nature different from contemporary men: they were creators and these are imitators. It is conjoined with it because nothing has been going on since the appearance of the ancestors except events whose recurrence periodically effaces their particularity" (*The Savage Mind* [English trans. 1966], 236). Lévi-Strauss is speaking of those cultures we hesitantly term primitive. There is nothing primitive about Pindar, but archaic thinking preserves, in a higher form, many elements of the primitive, and Lévi-Strauss throws light on Pindar's conception of those actions we call historical. The Battle of Salamis

can be seen as a particular event with new and even revolu-
tionary implications—for example, that the *thetes*, the lowest
free social class in Athens, whose muscle-power drove the
Greek ships against the Persian fleet, should not be denied
their share of political influence. There were those in Athens
who came to see Salamis in this way. For Pindar, however,
when he treats of Salamis in the fifth Isthmian ode, the recent
achievement of Aiginetan sailors in the battle, like the victory
of the Aiginetan athlete in whose honor the poem was written, falls into a recognizable pattern. Both are directly related,
as "end" or fulfillment (*telos*) to cause or origin (*arkha*), to the
heroic deeds of the island's ancestral heroes at Troy, the Aiakidai, sons and grandsons of the founding hero Aiakos, who
was planted by Zeus in the womb of the nymph Aigina.
Within a thinking of this sort, the new can have no disruptive
power. Neither history nor politics can get any hold on events
whose particularity is instantly and effortlessly absorbed by
the foundational myths and understood as proceeding from
them.

Perhaps this is too extreme a way of putting it, yet the
alien perspective it offers may still be salutary. If we hope to
get close to Pindar, we must first see how far from us he is.
To live imaginatively in the world of myth and legend does
not mean being blind to the events of the day: it can mean
seeing those events more profoundly. Pindar understood very
well what was happening around him in Greece. The first
Pythian ode shows that he grasped the connection between
the victories won by Sicilian princes over Carthage and Etruria
at the outer reaches of Hellas and the more celebrated battles
of Salamis and Plataia, in which mainland Greeks defeated
the might of Persia. In his eighth Pythian, last and greatest
of the many poems he wrote for Aigina, he contemplated (so
some still believe) the defeat of this old aristocratic society at

the hands of the arrogant new power of democratic Athens. We are warned not to find any "statement of political principle" here. No, there is something more valuable, both timely and timeless—the image of political tragedy held in the mirror of poetry.

> Men are we, and must grieve when even the Shade
> Of that which once was great, is passed away.

It follows from what I have said that this book looks for the Pindar who matters or could matter now. This does not mean modernizing Pindar.

All that remains is to thank those who have helped me. First to acknowledge is my gratitude to the general editor of this series, John Herington, whose vigilant eye neither vice nor virtue can escape. A man of letters no less than a scholar, he brought an ideal attention to my manuscript, sentence by sentence improving and reproving. Whatever has survived his disapproval I will no doubt come to regret. Another large obligation is to William Mullen, who also read my text searchingly and persuaded me to abandon some cherished errors. I first knew Mr. Mullen as in some sort my pupil, but the relation was soon reversed and I have been learning from him ever since. All who are familiar with his work on Pindar will perceive the extent of my debt—if "debt" can be made to cover a good deal of local pilfering and at least one case of wholesale robbery. Κοινὰ τὰ τῶν φίλων, can I lamely plead? What this book owes to Teresa Iverson is indicated, all too briefly, in the dedication. She has been in on the project from its bear-whelp beginnings to whatever form it may finally have achieved, guiding me, from her own fine sense of Pindar's poetry, to the way in which it could best be proposed to today's incurious world.

ABBREVIATIONS

Bundy
    Bundy, Elroy L. *Studia Pindarica I and II*. Berkeley, 1962.

Burton
    Burton, R. W. B. *Pindar's Pythian Odes*. Oxford, 1962.

Bury
    Bury, J. B. *The Nemean Odes of Pindar*. London, 1890.

    ———— *The Isthmian Odes of Pindar*. London, 1892.

Farnell
    Farnell, L. R. *The Works of Pindar II: Critical Commentary*. London, 1932.

Gildersleeve
    Gildersleeve, Basil L. *Pindar: The Olympian and Pythian Odes*. New York, 1890.

Slater
    Slater, W. J. *Lexicon to Pindar*. Berlin, 1969.

I THE PINDARIC VICTORY ODE

"FEW PEOPLE CARE FOR PINDAR NOW," GILBERT MURRAY WROTE around the turn of this century. From Germany some years later Wilamowitz said much the same thing and explained why: "His world is quite alien to us. Its customs, its thinking and aspirations we find unattractive if not offensive. He himself is no rich spirit." The poets agreed. "If Pindar bores us, we admit it," Eliot granted languidly. Pound was more vehement: "'Theban Eagle' be blowed. A dam'd rhetorician half the time. . . . The prize wind-bag of all ages." A forlorn hope, it must seem, to retrieve and commend to today's reader this unpopular poet who is also, everyone assures us, very difficult.

Pindar, I shall maintain, is for the most part not as difficult as he has been made out, but one real difficulty, and at the same time challenge, his work does present, though it is not of his making: only in a nominal sense has he ever been part of our tradition. Other Greek poets survived within a genre which they created or helped to establish. The prestige of the epic form carried Homer safely down the ages. Attic tragedy may differ in many ways from anything that moved across the later tragic stage, but something called tragedy persisted, at least intermittently, and some umbilical cord still binds us to the Athenian masters. Comedy too persists, however far it has diverged from the old comic form in which Aristophanes did his best work. So with the slighter genres, lyric, pastoral, epigram. But the "victory ode," the special branch of choric poetry by which Pindar is now chiefly represented, is another matter. High-flown, elaborately patterned poems written on commission to praise a victorious boxer or wrestler and assure him that he has scaled the heights of mortal achievement, the encomiastic element combined with bits of gnomic wisdom and seemingly personal utterance and leading out to passages of myth not always obviously related to the occasion and presented in concentrated lyrical form—the whole gallimaufry set to the most intricate meters in Greek and designed to be sung and danced by a chorus of citizens: this is a literary oddity the like of which the world has not seen again. Not surprisingly it enjoyed a fairly limited life span. Created or developed by Simonides (born mid-sixth century B.C.), it was brought to full flower by Pindar and his younger contemporary Bacchylides in the early and middle fifth century, by the end of which it was already obsolete. When Pindar's odes were collected and studied in Alexandria in the third century B.C., they were stripped of whatever musical and choreographical notation must originally have accompanied them and the sense of the occasion was lost—a whole people bound together by the intense communal life of the old city-state and joyfully united to pay homage to a young athletic hero. It is true that tragedy, as a vital form, did not survive the fifth century either, but tragedies continued to be performed and indeed written. The victory ode did not; only the texts survived, and the bare words must have seemed very bare indeed, their rapturous tone scarcely comprehensible, their festal brightness all gone flat. Imagine watching an opera singer on the television screen with the sound turned off: the man's mouth opens and shuts, he is obviously in a state of great excitement, but what is he excited about?

Pindar continued to be read and studied since he was now part of the canon, first of the nine lyric poets, *regnator lyricae cohortis*, as a Roman writer called him. Studied, but not perhaps much loved, and not deeply understood. A false or at least misleading conception of his poetry took hold and was to last through the centuries, a view that emphasized his grandeur, his sublimity, at the expense of his other virtues. A poet of the *Greek Anthology* described him as "the powerful [or heavy] smith of finely wrought verses" (7.34) and Horace, in an influential ode, compared him to a river which plunges down the mountains and overflows its banks: "mighty-mouthed he seethes and rushes on." Horace was a sensitive literary critic and may well have been aware that he was giving a one-sided picture (the purpose of the ode is to plead that, lacking Pindar's lofty powers, he cannot write a poem praising the Emperor's military exploits). As the old poetry of Greece became increasingly remote, however, less sensitive readers may have seen only this side of his genius, sometimes praising it—Quintilian speaks of his grandeur, "the full stream of his eloquence"—sometimes criticizing. The ancient scholia or commentaries on Pindar, that jumble of genuine learning and classroom parsing, reveal a good deal of discomfort with what is felt to be the poet's hyperbolic, catachrestic diction and metaphors.

When, with the Renaissance, Pindar surfaced again in the West, the literary world, not knowing what else to do with this extraordinary body of work, took over the judgment of later antiquity or tried to imitate the external features of Pindaric poetry without understanding the spirit. Rabelais describes a French Holofernes (who says "Nous transfretons la Sequane au dilucule" when he means cross the Seine at dawn) as "pindarizing," and Ronsard laboriously pindarized his way through fourteen odes, ordinary French stanzas parceled up into strophes, antistrophes and epodes—"thrice twisted in a Theban ply," he fondly supposed. A generation later in Italy, Chiabrera, with his *Canzoni Eroiche*, Pindaric in aspiration though not attempting triadic form, achieved a somewhat greater energy and elevation, but by then the fatal confusion between classical and neoclassical or classicist had set in—antiquity on stilts, the turbulence of life frozen into marble nobility—and was to obscure our vision of the ancient world for centuries. England can offer something more solid with Jonson's triadic ode for Sir Henry Morison, but—or rather because—the inspiration is Horatian, not Pindaric. More influential and more representative of the poet Pindar was thought to be were the *Pindarique Odes* of Abraham Cowley (1656), metrically irregular compositions going all out for fougue and foaming slightly at the mouth. Pindar in an English habit, Cowley claimed. A glimpse of something very different had emerged a few years earlier with the Latin ode in free Pindaric form which Milton wrote for the Oxford librarian Rous. This poem, which has never received the attention it deserves, suggests that Milton saw in Pindar a deft, sophisticated artist rather than the thundering or frantic rhapsode of tradition. The contrast between the subject of the poem (a mislaid book) and the gravity of the manner is urbane, even witty, and there are passages which make one wish that Milton had left us a translation of an ode. These lines to Rous, for example:

> Aeternorum operum custos fidelis,
> Quaestorque gazae nobilioris
> Quam cui praefuit Ion,
> Clarus Erechtheides,
> Opulenta dei per templa parentis
> Fulvosque tripodas, donaque Delphica,
> Ion Actaea genitus Creusa.

Faithful warden of immortal works, treasurer charged with wealth nobler than the golden tripods and Delphic offerings over which the famous scion Erechtheus presided in the rich temples of his divine father—Ion, child of Attic Creusa.

Milton had of course studied Pindar closely and possessed an exceptional feeling for Greek. Gray, however, in the next century, was also a learned poet and he too admired Pindar, yet he cannot get beyond the conventional picture. What he sees in Pindar ("Sailing with supreme dominion / Through the azure deep of air") is still only the lofty port, the sublimity. In one form or another this Pindar lives on today, and classicists will sometimes pause to show their reading by comparing him to Gerard Hopkins.

Only in Germany is the story somewhat different thanks to one great poet, Hölderlin, who reached deeply enough into Pindar to write Pindaric odes of his own. The series of translations which he made around 1800 are word for word, bone-literal, yet at their best they are more than interlinear trots. Hölderlin may have set out to lay bare the kinship between the German and Greek languages, but it seems likely that in seeking to come close to Pindar he saw how distant he was and faced, as few have done, the essential otherness of the Greek. However, neither Hölderlin's translation nor the odes he wrote later were known till the early twentieth century, hence their influence on Pindaric studies has been limited.

The fact is that, with these rare exceptions, the Theban eagle has never been a familiar sight in our skies; he has been mewed up in the dust and silence of libraries. Without scholarship, no classical text could survive and be read, but scholarship alone cannot preserve a poet as a vital presence. That is the task of poets and good readers of poetry from generation to generation. If Homer and Virgil and Horace have (until yesterday) been household figures, it is because they lived on in our poetry through allusion, imitation, and translation. This did not happen with Pindar and in consequence he has remained a marginal figure in our tradition.

It would be a mistake, of course, to suggest that these long-standing judgments are entirely wrong. Pindar's poetry is indeed often very grand,

Vested in the serious fold of majesty,

but it is a great deal else too. Certainly he is a strong poet, but his strength is not at all like that of Hopkins, whose thudding hammer-blows are decidedly un-Pindaric; in his massive show of force Hopkins is if anything more Aeschylean. Pindar is a strong poet, yes, but also as light on his toes as the dancers who moved to his syllables. His poetry can be solemn and sometimes remote, yes again, but it is also (to borrow more words from Wallace Stevens) "crested / With every prodigal, familiar fire." We have only to think of the joyful occasions for which Pindar's victory odes were composed to realize that something *must* be wrong with the way people have so often spoken of him. Pindar the preacher, for instance. (A nineteenth-century fiction, this.) Who wanted a preacher at such a time? What place was there for the "heavy earnestness" which a distinguished German critic attributes to him? Or for the desperate obscurity some have found in his work?

It is satisfactory to be able to report that some new Pindars have recently emerged. There is Pindar the great technician, master of the intricate epinician genre. We will be looking at this influential figure in a moment. Still more promising, to my mind, is the Pindar offered by an acute verbal critic, M. S. Silk: Pindar the "master of the delicate style."

Seeking to reclaim Spenser from his reputation, C. S. Lewis once proposed replacing the epithets usually applied to that poet with a new set. Not Italianate, voluptuous, elfin, decorative Spenser; but rather English, churchwardenly, manly, thrifty Spenser. In the same spirit I would propose not sublime, heavy, earnest, Beethovian Pindar, but delicate, light-footed, deft, Mozartian Pindar. I am anticipating, however, and need to take a few steps back in order to retrace briefly but in a more orderly fashion the stages of the recovery or possibility of recovering a truer picture of this poet.

○ ○ ○

The modern study of Pindar may be said to begin in the second decade of the nineteenth century with the great edition of Boeckh and Dissen which laid the foundations of Pindaric scholarship and, on a far more tentative level, criticism. From the start, as David C. Young has shown in a survey of this field, the cardinal problem was that of unity. How does a Pindaric ode hang together, what is the relation of its seemingly unconnected elements? The spectacle of a series of learned men searching for something that neither their training nor their talents qualified them to recognize, poetic unity, is dispiriting; the results of their labors, not surprisingly, are from the critical point of view meager. Dissen proposed that every ode contains a "basic thought," some maxim or moral saying which can be extracted from it and in the light of which it can be interpreted. This unpromising notion proved all too influential: refined and elaborated in various ways, it was pursued through much of the century. Some real progress was made, but further advance was cut short, embarrassingly enough, by the entry into this field of one of the most imposing figures in classical scholarship. Wilamowitz' published work on Pindar, beginning in the mid-eighties and extending over more than three decades, now belongs to history (pretty recent history, though; a book like C. M. Bowra's *Pindar* of 1964 is still heavily indebted) and would have little place in a work of this sort were it not that to a disquieting extent the contemporary approach to Pindar is a reaction against Wilamowitz. The most recent German edition of Pindar, Erich Thummer's *Isthmischen Gedichte* of 1968–69, quotes and rebuts Wilamowitz on almost every other page.

Wilamowitz seems not to have thought highly of Pindar's poetry, despite the fine purple patches it contains, and he tacitly abandoned the search for unity, treating the odes primarily as historical documents. A good deal of what he derived from them can unfortunately only be described as historical romancing—as when we see Pindar, home from his sojourn in the Sicilian courts and by now a wealthy man, defending himself against Theban accusations of currying favor with tyrants. Why a victor should pay Pindar to write an ode in which the poet could air his private problems is never explained. Wilamowitz' *Pindaros* (1922) has good incidental things to say about Pindar, and on aspects of Greek culture reflected in his poetry there is still much to learn from it; but for an understanding of the poems as works of art the book is little better than useless.

The historicizing approach, as I said, now belongs to history, and the Pindar we read today is a very different figure— or rather, the epinician ode as we read it today is a very different poem—for attention has profitably shifted from the poet to his work, from attendant historical or biographical circumstance to the epinician genre. The odes are now seen to be governed by what Elroy L. Bundy—to concentrate the reaction in the person of its most influential spokesman— called a "grammar of choral style." What is needed, Bundy declared in his *Studia Pindarica* (two brief, densely argued papers published in 1962), is "a thorough study of conventional themes, motives and sequences in choral poetry." How radical a challenge he posed to the approaches hitherto held in honor may be judged by a single representative passage. We forget, Bundy wrote, that

> this is an oral, public, epideictic literature dedicated to the single purpose of eulogizing men and communities; that these eulogies are concentrated upon athletic achievement; that the environment thus created is hostile to an allusiveness that would strain the powers of a listening audience, hostile to personal, religious, political, philosophical and historical references that might interest the poet but do nothing to enhance the glory of a given patron, hostile to abruptness in transitions, to gross irrelevance, to lengthy sermonizing, to literary scandals and embarrassments, hostile in short to all the characteristics of style and temper that we ascribe to Pindar. (II.35)

This redirection was variously fruitful. It cleared away many hardened errors of interpretation and by showing how dexterously Pindar handled the conventions of his intricate form gave us, virtually for the first time, a clear picture of what that form was. A path to the odes now lay open. The dangers of Bundy's approach were clear from the start, and the better critics have not been blind to them: specifically, in clearing away so much it left one wondering if what remained could be worth reading, and what it offered was not so much Pindar the great poet as Pindar the great technician. And yet, inevitably perhaps in a technological age, the more mechanical side of Bundy's work has proved all too influential and brought a somewhat excessive concern with the epinician genre itself—this complicated piece of ancient mechanism we have so cleverly uncovered—and critics delight to scrutinize and catalogue its various parts, taking it to pieces to find out how the thing works. Surely, though, unless we hope to compose epinician odes ourselves, it cannot be the genre which primarily concerns us but what Pindar did with it. It is the odes that matter, the individual poems which, for all their formal affinities, have their own unique tone and atmosphere and color. Pindar's clients, the victorious athletes he was commissioned to praise, were after all very diverse people. An unknown boy from an ancient town like Orkhomenos, rich in legend and sacred association, and a glittering Sicilian magnate with a great deal of money but no ancestral lore to his name: the genre could accommodate them both, but they required very different treatment. So too did the places they came from and yet, although "praise of the victor's homeland" is now catalogued as an epinician topic, we are curiously reluctant about allowing that Pindar actually knew the places he praised. He will announce in an ode that he "has come" to the victor's city. Wilamowitz used such passages, quite illicitly, to plot Pindar's travels; we now list them as examples of the "arrival motif" and remind ourselves that he "came" only by poetic convention. Sometimes no doubt this was the case, but often he must really have gone to a city with his ode, perhaps only roughed out so that he could build bits of local color and legend into it when he had wandered about and drunk in the tone of the place. In an interesting note on Olympian 7, where Pindar brilliantly tells how the victor's birthplace, the island of Rhodes, came into existence, the scholiast remarks that since no historical accounts existed in Pindar's day poets had to gather their information from local antiquaries and old men "who could call on Time as witness to the accuracy of their knowledge." With a few vivid strokes Pindar can make us see a place, its physical aspect or its inner, spiritual landscape: Orkhomenos with its river and fine horses grazing in the meadows nearby, the "templed hill" of Akragas (so Lattimore, charmingly), the "rich and sacred street of his ancestors" where an Aiginetan victor lived, his house set between two shrines to Herakles, or, finest of all, the ceremonial Paved Way in Cyrene down which the poet leads us to the agora, at one corner of which is the tomb of the ancestral hero, "blessed while he dwelled among men and now a dread presence." These pictures are among the beauties of Pindaric poetry and even if we think they are incidental it is no mark of sound criticism to ignore them.

Since Pindar was very successful in his day, we must suppose that he fully met the requirements of his genre; and certainly we should know in some detail what those requirements were. He did the job he was paid for, did it handsomely and in the way required by convention. But if there is to be any talk of Pindar the great poet, he must have done *more* than the victory ode required, more for instance than his contemporary Bacchylides did with the genre. This *don gratuit*, this supererogatory largesse, should claim our fullest attention. I do not at all mean that we should expect to find Pindar inserting into an ode matter irrelevant to his encomiastic task; rather, in celebrating the victor (celebration is a mode of poetry) he is likely to be celebrating a whole way of life, the special virtues and local features and traditions and legends and landscapes that lie around and behind the present moment of triumph. In praising a man and his place, Pindar creates a world. There was more than enough room within the compass of the victory ode for his sense of life to find expression there, his vision of man and reality. And surely, sometimes, his response (his *poetic* response) to the great issues of the day. Yet here again, overreacting against Wilamowitz, who found politics cropping up everywhere, we do

our best to keep them out wherever we can and credit Pindar
with an exclusive and excluding formal purity. In his devotion
to the genre and its requirements, he apparently did not
pause to reflect on so large a matter as the transformation of
Greek life brought about by the rapid expansion of Athenian
power, even when he was addressing a community that was
feeling the rough edge of Athenian power. Were the odes
really composed in a generic vacuum?

There may after all be something to learn from older approaches to the poet, aspects of his genius that we in these
rigorous days seem blind to. In the prelude to Isthmian 5
Pindar invokes—and more than half invents, from a shadowy
personage in Hesiod—a goddess called Theia, Divine One.
Mother of the Sun, her presence is felt in the magic brightness
of gold and the pulse and glitter of impassioned spectacle—
in racing ships or the headlong contest of chariots. This "momentary goddess" is an incarnation of the more than mortal
light or *aigla* which, for Pindar, irradiates mortal affairs in the
hour of victory. Older critics like Lewis Farnell and Wilamowitz devoted eloquent words to this mysterious figure, finding in her a genuine expression of Greek religious feeling and
even of Pindar's own beliefs. (This is a critical red herring, of
course; we are not concerned with what Pindar the man may
have believed but with what his poetry believes and finds
important.) Consult the latest commentary on the Isthmians,
that of Erich Thummer, and you find no suggestion that this
may be a passage worth pondering. The reader is in fact told
not to attach "any special weight" to it and is warned against
Wilamowitz' overestimation of this and other preludes. What
we have here is simply . . . a prelude. It does its epinician job
by flashing brilliantly before our eyes for a moment and then
gives way to the true and only subject of the ode (and now

for a draft of the pure milk of Bundy), "praise of the victor, of his homeland, his family, and his trainer."

We have learned from recent studies that the victory ode is a highly disciplined form with its special conventions, its recurrent, expected features. It does not take long to recognize these things, once one has been alerted to their presence and function, and to enjoy the poet's skill in handling them and see how they are used as structural principles of composition. The victory ode, one comes to realize, is more like a classical symphony, or more exactly perhaps a classical sonata, than like any poetry written since the Romantic period. It differs from most modern poetry in this respect too, that it is always occasional, and to understand why Pindar's odes are as they are we must do what we can (it is not much) to picture the occasions they served. So and so has gained a victory in one of the four great games, Olympian, Pythian, Nemean, or Isthmian. His triumph will be celebrated on the evening of the day with a brief traditional or impromptu song, but something more solid and more splendid is needed if the achievement is to be fittingly memorialized. So the victor or his family commission a poet to compose a celebratory ode which will be performed later on at home. In due course the great day arrives and we must imagine the whole community united in a state of joyful anticipation, for victory in one of the major games is not simply a family affair but a civic triumph, and the victor will enjoy certain privileges in his township for life. The poet will often be there in person to conduct the performance, or he may have sent the ode and left the performance in the hands of a local chorus master.

Several weeks of rehearsal will be needed, for this is a complex, composite art, with intricately patterned words to be
danced and sung to the music of flute or lyre. Pindar speaks
in his third Olympian of "fitting the voice of festal splendor
to the Doric sandal." The chorus is composed of young men
of the region, trained from earliest youth in the art of choral
dancing, as every educated Greek was, and the public too
will know more or less what to look for, in the way that a
musically literate person knows what to look for in a piece of
classical music.

Certain elements must obviously always be included. The
victor's name has to be announced, the festival at which he
competed and the type of contest he won. Given the close tie
binding a man to his family or clan and to his city, they too
must receive their due honor. Other features we would not
necessarily expect are also required; we will be looking at
some of them in the course of this chapter and more closely
in the readings of individual poems which follow. Some features we might expect we do not find, or only very sparingly.
About the contest itself almost nothing is said, unless there
was some special reason for it. Fortunately enough, the genre
did not require Pindar to report that "our man was running
strongly in second place on the inside track, but then with
the final lap. . . ."

Let us look at an ode and see how the poet carries out
his commission. He begins Pythian 9 with a poetic equivalent
of the actual proclamation of victory made immediately after
the contest:

I long to proclaim him!
    He took the Pythian crown, a bronzeshield runner—
and the Graces join in my cry

that garlands Kyrána:
this fortunate man Telesíkrates.*

The job is deftly done in the Greek with four sonorous lines
stating the contest (the race in armor), the name of the festival, the victor's name, and the name of his city, Kyrana (Cyrene, in Libya). Four essential elements, and a fifth: the
credentials of the poet. He can be trusted to praise the victor
fittingly since he is inspired by the Graces, the goddesses
who, with the Muses, preside over victory celebration.

Since these and other elements must always be included,
the poet has to come up with novel ways of presenting them.
Variation plays a crucial role in these poems whose immediate
task is always the same. We learn to take pleasure in the poet's
skill in ringing the changes on his generic constants, even
when the material itself strikes us as out of place in lyric
poetry. Take the so-called victory list. A man who scored in
one of the great games was likely to have had other victories
to his credit; often he came from an athletically successful
family, and the poet was required—it would have been part
of his commission—to work these various triumphs into the
ode. They could not just be slipped in; they had to stand out
in bold glorious relief. Nor could they simply be listed—"He
won the footrace at A and B and his brother won the boxing
match at C," and so forth. The thing had to be done artisti-
cally. Pindar seems to have relished the task of composing
these victorious catalogues, but although he handles them
with great skill they are a feature of the odes which the modern reader has to learn to enjoy. It is a lesson worth learning

*Greek proper names are accented, in the translations of passages of Pin-
dar, merely to indicate where the stress conventionally falls in English; these
are not the Greek accents and are meant to help the reader catch the rhythm
of a line.

all the same, for it opens a way not only to aspects of Pindaric
and other classical poetry but of our own traditional poetry
which, since the Romantic period, we have not been at home
with. Milton and Pope, for instance, are not only great poets,
they are great poetic craftsmen who delight in and should
delight us with their consummate virtuosity. So too Pindar,
who displays his virtuosity when he heightens the bare statement "He won in the Nemean games" into this:

> Leaves from the Lion's Field thatched his brow
> the day he won
> in the shadow of the immemorial hills of Phleious.
> (Nemean 6.42 ff.)

(The Nemean valley, near the town of Phleious, was where
Herakles killed the Nemean lion, one of his traditional labors.)
Sometimes Pindar is content with kennings which we find at
best ingenious, as when he announces that the victor has won
"a warm remedy against chilly winds" (Olympian 9.97; the
prize was a woolen jacket). Often he circumvents our preju-
dices successfully—in these lines, surely, for a victor in the
Athenian games:

> Sweetly
> preludial voices hailed his triumph at Athens
> twice. And their fired earth brought the olive's fruit
> to this brave land of Hera
> in the great jar's patterned hold.
> (Nemean 10.33 ff.)

The prize was a richly decorated amphora filled with olive oil.
The vessel is broken down into its constituent parts—the
earth out of which it was made, the fruit of the olive which
fills it, the painted round of its circumference. Hera's land is
Argos where the victor came from. Pindar is doing here what

the poet, Santayana said, must always do, disintegrating "the fictions of common perception into their sensuous elements" and recreating them in poetry's special terms to produce the sudden shock of a thing truly seen. This may seem strangely modern. Too modern for Pindar? Not necessarily. The resources of poetry have always been available to poets, even if criticism has been tardy in coming up with the terms to describe them.

The best-known and most popular feature of the Pindaric ode is the myth, though in fact by no means all odes contain a myth; nine out of the forty-five do not. They provide the occasion for some of the most dazzling poetry in Greek, but like most things in Pindar they have often puzzled his readers. Ancient criticism got us off to a bad start by regularly referring to the myths as "digressions." Two things have in particular been much canvassed, the way in which they are narrated and their relation to the victor. Both questions can best be taken in the context of particular poems, but it will be helpful to try to clear up a few points in advance.

Pindar tells a story not in chronological sequence of events but by presenting a series of lyrical moments or pictures, cutting swiftly from one to another and omitting narrative links in order to achieve the maximum concentration. Often he will start with an exciting moment near the end of the story. In Pythian 9, after the initial proclamation of the victor, he relates how in the primal days Apollo brought the nymph Kyrana to the place where her future city would arise and there made her his bride. This is the high moment of the myth and hence comes first. Pindar then moves back in time to tell us who Kyrana was, how Apollo first saw her, and after a prophecy about her future he tracks forward again and ends with another account of her marriage with the god. This mode of composition, circular rather than linear and normally re-

gressive, is now known as ring-composition; Kyrana's story
begins with her marriage and rounds back to the same
event—the ring has closed on itself.

The general purpose of myth, in Pindar's odes as in almost all high Greek poetry and in the archaic poetry of other
times and places, is to set the particular, nonrecurrent event—
here a victory in the games—in relation to an event in the
permanent, paradigmatic world of the gods and heroes which
makes it understandable. The bearing of the individual myth
on this or that ode has given rise to much discussion, more
perhaps than is needed since usually there is a clear enough
formal or official link to the athlete whose triumph is being
celebrated. The myth may relate directly to him (in Olympian
6 the victor was a prophet, so Pindar tells the story of the
founder of his clan who was also a prophet), or to an event
in his family history (the myth in Nemean 10 concerns the
semidivine heroes Kastor and Polydeukes who were once entertained by an ancestor of the victor; since they were patrons
of the games, the family has been athletically successful ever
since). Sometimes the myth is related to the victor's homeland
(the victor in Olympian 7 came from Rhodes and the myth
relates three crucial moments in the island's history), sometimes to the place where the victory was gained (the myth in
Olympian 3 describes how Herakles founded the Olympian
games). There is naturally more to it than this, and the function of the myth is sometimes genuinely obscure—to us at
least. The best course is to look for some general consonance
without trying to set up any mechanical point-for-point correspondence, leaving the mind free to ponder the deeper re-
lations which bind the myth to its ode. I spoke of the formal
or official connection, but this is sometimes no more than the
bone thrown to the dog to allow the burglar to get on with

his job undisturbed, to use Eliot's figure. Pindar's finest myths work in strange ways, most wonderfully when they trace the present moment of victory back to the foundational event which brought it about. This event—a sacred marriage between a god and the ancestral heroine of the victor's city it may be, or some great deed of bravery performed by an ances-tor—is the origin of today's triumph, the seed from which it grew. And the movement goes two ways, not only from foun-dational event to present victory but back or rather *down*, from present victory to foundational event, a path to which now lies open. What grants the enormous joy breathing through the odes, before which we stand abashed and awed, is that for a brief stretch of profane time a place here on earth is bathed in the sacred light of the origins. But this leads straight to Pindar's deeps and we are not yet ready to venture into those mysterious regions.

Like myth, gnomic sentences and pithy bits of proverbial wisdom are found, inserted at strategic points, throughout the odes, as in all high Greek poetry; they too are a means of understanding the local and particular in the timeless terms of general truth. Pindar will often introduce his sententiae in the first person. "I will be small among the small, great among the great," he says in Pythian 3, and goes on to speak of what would happen if the gods should grant him wealth. He is not talking about himself here or inopportunely introducing his financial expectations. In such passages the first person means no more than "one," any man—the "first person in-definite," it has been neatly termed. Another very common and still more neutral function of the first person is to mark a transition from one part of the ode to another. In Olympian 8, after a passage in praise of the victor, the poet declares: "But I must awaken memory to tell"—and he goes on to

praise the man's family. In Nemean 10, having celebrated the
victor's homeland, he protests that there is simply too much
to say on the subject:

> Too much for my tongue's telling
> all the fine things this Argive precinct holds!

and turns to the victor himself. The first person singular
serves its functional purpose of signaling a new movement
even when it seems to record a personal experience requiring
attention in its own right.

In addition to these functional usages of the first person,
there are many passages where we hear the poet himself in
one of his several roles, as participant in and director of the
performance (in reality or by convention), and as guest-friend
of the victor whose achievement he is eager to praise. Our
knowledge of what happened on these ancient occasions is
so limited that there is often no way of deciding whether we
hear the poet himself or the chorus among whom he is stationed. The bare text does not need to be explicit here since
performance would have made the matter plain. There is no
difficulty when, at the start of Isthmian 1, written for a Theban victor, he addresses Theba, ancestral heroine of their city,
as "my mother." This is Pindar the Theban poet. But what of
Nemean 3 where he begins by speaking of the Muse as "our
mother"? We assume that this is a choral utterance, but then
the poet distinguishes himself from the chorus by describing
them as they stand by the bank of their river waiting for the
Muse's voice, or in other words the poet's song. The matter
could be pursued (and is being pursued) in much greater
detail, but perhaps all that needs be said here is that we
should be on our guard against two opposing errors. We
should not bluntly say "This is Pindar speaking" whenever
we come across a personal pronoun. Nor should we banish

him from the odes or be too zealous about finding a strictly epinician function for every personal utterance. When at the end of Isthmian 6 Pindar says of the victor and his father:

> I will give them a draft of the holy water of Dirka
> which the daughters of Memory golden-robed
> made to spring by the walled city of Kadmos

he is doing two things which we should not try to distinguish. He is stating his poetic credentials, a regular epinician element; the victor can be assured that the praise he is getting, drawn from the very source of all poetry, will be of the highest quality. Pindar is also asserting, with proper pride, the sacrality of his poetic calling. Great artists are not always modest little people.

This account of the victory ode has been brief, deliberately so. Pindaric specialists have debated each of the topics here discussed at great length; but I have found that a good many of them are less troublesome than they have been made out to be in the scholarly literature. In any case, the beginner—and the general reader—would be well advised to take them in stride. Moreover, paying undue attention to the conventional and generic can result in underplaying what may be uniquely Pindaric or, in other words, innovative. When a major artist makes use of an existing form he does not simply follow the rules and leave the thing as he found it. He is more likely to reshape it to his own ends. In Bacchylides one senses a modest, somewhat anonymous performer; when you commissioned an ode from him, you probably got more or less what you expected, a finely crafted decently conventional poem. I suspect that the more enterprising people who engaged Pindar's services did so knowing full well that there was no telling what to expect. That was the wonder of the man.

○ ○ ○

We should master the grammar of choral lyric, learning its rules so well that we internalize them and half "forget" them: in order to leave our attention free for what may be specially even uniquely Pindaric, for the strange and, yes, *difficult* things his poetry has to offer. His reputation as a difficult poet may not, after all, be wholly undeserved; long-standing judgments are seldom quite without foundation. There must be something to Voltaire's gibe (everyone praises Pindar because no one understands him) and to Cowley's claim that if someone translated Pindar word for word "it would be thought that one madman had translated another." Even the *débordements* of the seventeenth- and eighteenth-century Pindarique ode must reflect some quality in the original, something that the Greek scholiasts were pointing to when they censured the poet's metaphors as harsh and dithyrambic. Surely it *is* very odd to say of a victor:

> that evening by Kastalia's fountain
> he flamed with the clamor of the Graces
>
> (Nemean 6.37 f.)

and the oddity is not removed by noting that the verb is here conventional. Pindar's diction is often heightened to a point well beyond the expected hyperbole of praise. He starts one ode (Olympian 9) by saying that the brief traditional song hailing the victor does well enough for the immediate occasion but that if his achievement is to be celebrated properly something more is needed. He goes on (I quote from the translation of Frank Nisetich to show that I am not forcing the text to my argument):

> But now
> let the long-range bow of the Muses aim

at Zeus himself, lord of crimson lightning,
and let its arrows rain upon
the sacred height of Elis. . . .

Then he turns to the victor's city. Praise her, he cries,

for her triumphs
bursting in bloom
by Kastalia's stream. . . .

So I make this city blaze,
fuel to my impetuous song,
this town I love.

The expression, here and often elsewhere, is not just highly
energetic; it is wrought to such a pitch of intensity and excitement that to the outsider it can well appear slightly mad.
Consider the way Pindar praises his victors. They paid him
to praise them, of course, and expected their poet to tell them
and the world at large that by coming in first in the four
hundred yards they had done something quite out of the ordinary. One can't help feeling, all the same, that the height
at which he chose to pitch it must sometimes have made them
wonder if what they had done quite matched the words that
the poet had devised. Bacchylides is content to tell his victors
that their achievement is "laid up on high with the gods"
(ode 9.82 ff.) and that their fame will live on after death
(13.63 f.). Sometimes Pindar does not say much more than
this even though, being a stronger poet, he says it more powerfully. One victor "has gone to the top of man's endeavor"
(Nemean 3.20); to another he says "for a mortal there is no
further peak to reach" (Nemean 9.47). He strikes a stranger,
more rapturous note when he says that the victor "casts anchor on the farthest shores of joy" (Isthmian 6.12 f.). Stranger
still, to our ears, what he says on two occasions: "Do not try

to be God" (Olympian 5.24, Isthmian 5.14). He is not preaching prudence to his triumphant young men or warning them to go no further but telling them how staggeringly far they have come. They have momentarily entered a condition only just short of the unending felicity of the immortals. In his last and greatest poem he sees a light playing round the victor that is almost unearthly, *aigla diosdotos*, a radiance granted by Zeus.

Pindar's is a world of straddling energy and splendor, so brilliantly lit that to untutored eyes it can seem to glare. He is not hysterical or feverish; you do not have the uncomfortable sense, as you often do with a poet like Tasso, that his temperature is several degrees above normal. His pulse is steady. This is where as a poet he lives and is at home, a world where everything and everyone is *au comble du paraître*, standing before us in the plenitude of their being. Here is a golden wine bowl, *phialan khrusōi pephrikuian*. The verb (*phrissein*) means to shiver or shudder and we should let it carry its full force here. This bowl, as Pindar sees it, is not simply gleaming or glittering with gold, as translators are mostly content to write, but shuddering: *phialam auro horrentem*. Your father would praise you if he were still alive, Pindar tells one victor. But no, what the Greek says is "if he were still warmed by the raging Sun" (Nemean 4.13 f.). Soldiers in battle "break wounds" (Nemean 8.29) in the hot flesh of their enemies— "tear," everyone translates. Fire rises from an altar, "kicking the heavens with savory smoke of sacrifice" (Isthmian 4.66). Most translators prefer to write "lashing" or the like. A constant tendency of our tradition of interpretation from ancient times to today has been to tone down and tame this passionate diction.

I spoke just now of the outsider. The fact is that we are all outsiders with Pindar, in a sense and to a degree that we are not with Homer and the dramatists: outside his genre, outside the occasions for which his poems were composed. We do not of course know anything directly about these occasions; we cannot imagine ourselves part of those small Greek townships bound together (often torn apart) by their intense communal life and far more than normally bound by the burning desire to pay homage to the young athlete home from Delphi or Olympia with his simple but infinitely precious wreath. If by some miracle we could be transported to one of those distant celebrations I suspect we might find the whole thing entirely too much for us. "We would not dare to place ourselves in Renaissance circumstances," Nietzsche once wrote; "our nerves could not support that reality, not to mention our muscles" (*Twilight of the Idols*, IX.37). Although we are often warned against reading modern attitudes into the classical world, we still tend to assume—it is a lazy assumption—that the senses work in roughly the same way at all times and that despite cultural differences "reality" remains more or less constant. We need something like an archaeology of the emotions or senses to help us to understand the work of other ages, some way of taking the pulse of a period that would explain (to move nearer home) what it was in the world of Elizabeth and James which called for a diction not simply ebullient but constantly straining at the limits of expression ("Enrobe the roaring waters with my silks"—what a way for a merchant to speak of shipwreck!), and only a century later was content with the chastened speech of the age of Queen Anne.

Pindar's occasions have gone beyond recall; his odes remain and they are what concern us. They took fire, we must suppose, from those occasions while themselves greatly contributing to the blaze. As a means of getting a closer hold on this poetry—which in the days before we became grammar-

149,078

ians of choral lyric made some people wonder if Pindar was quite in his right mind—I propose to look at a single puzzling feature of his diction which turns up rather often: the way he uses what appears to be the language of love and sexual desire to convey the victor's relation to victory. In the first Olympian Pindar says, literally, that a racehorse "mingled his master with power [or victory]" (*kratei . . . prosemeixe despotan*). The verb *meignumi*, in its simple or compounded forms, is something of a favorite with Pindar. Meaning mix or mingle, it is used in Greek of various forms of contact or union, including sexual union. What does it mean here? "Brought power unto his master," the Loeb translator, Sandys, thinks; "brought success to his master," Slater agrees. Gildersleeve, the finest Pindaric commentator ("It is hardly possible to go wrong," he wrote, "in pressing Pindar's vocabulary until the blood comes"), has this to say: "The concrete, personal *meignumi* is common in Pindar, and must have its rights of contact. Here, 'brought to victory's embrace.' 'Wedded,' 'clasped,' 'embraced,' 'encircled,' will answer for many cases." Following Gildersleeve's lead, Nisetich gets the sense right though he hardly makes poetry of it: the horse "put his lord in the embrace of power." Victory, it seems, is (like?) an amorous bride.

This erotic diction or imagery is sometimes so clear that it cannot be concealed, though some have tried to dull its force. Of one young athlete Pindar says that he fell twice into the arms of victory and, literally, touched elaborately wrought song (Nemean 5.42). Sandys demurely prefers to let him fall into "the lap of victory" and "win" song. Farnell acknowledges "the voluptuous phrase" but is quick to warn us that "it is doubtful whether . . . the amorous idea is vividly present." A more robust commentator, J. B. Bury, says that the boy "enjoyed the embraces of . . . Victory" and suggests that the verb *touch* was "used by poets of the touches of amorous encounters." Nisetich, following this hint or perhaps simply guided by his own instinct, gives us—for the first time, I believe, in translation—what may be the true sense of the Greek:

> You, Euthymenes,
>   twice taken into the arms of Victory
> at Aigina, have known the embrace
> > of elaborate song.

A few lines later, of another victory, Nisetich translates:

> He vanquished those of his age
>   who came against him, at home
> and in the lovely arms of Megara.

(The victor, an Aiginetan, won victory as his bride just as in the myth his ancestor Peleus won Thetis.) The last line is a real recovery. The brown varnish has been scraped off to let us see the startlingly bright colors that were hidden all the time just beneath. The Greek is normally taken to mean that the boy won "in the beautiful-valley-by-the hill of Nisos" (*Nisou . . . en euangkei lophōi*), periphrastic for Megara. But the root element here, *angk-*, means primarily not a valley but anything curved or rounded and it occurred just before in the phrase about the arms of victory (*Nikas en angkōnessi*).

The sexual overtones found in the imagery sometimes pass over into the action of a poem, nowhere so explicitly as in the tenth Pythian, composed when Pindar was twenty. The ode sets up a relation between the joy of the festal occasion and the greater joy of the Hyperboreans, that legendary people who live, free from the cares of mortality, "beyond the North Wind." The official point is that no one, not even a victor, can experience that order of well-being. There are, however, a number of similarities between the two worlds

which go some way to bridging the gap. The Hyperboreans
are described as blessed, *makares*; Thessaly, the victor's home,
is also blessed. We see the Hyperboreans enjoying their privileged estate, crowned with golden leaves (the victor is also
crowned), as girls dance to the music of flute and lyre and
the whole place quivers or trembles with the flash of limbs
and the call of the instruments. There is dancing and singing
in Thessaly too as the chorus pours forth the poet's lovely
song beside the banks of the Peneios and the poet expresses
the hope that his ode will make the victor wonderful (*thaēton*)
in the eyes of the young men and their elders, an object too
of fond concern to girls. "Different loves excite the heart,"
Pindar goes on, using a verb often used of sexual excitement.
The erotic note, the sense that the victor is the focus of mark-
edly sexual attention, is strongly even disconcertingly emphasized by a moment earlier on in the myth. When we first
see them, the Hyperboreans are busy with a great sacrifice to
Apollo, a hecatomb of asses. The god enjoys the spectacle
"and laughs as he sees their beasts' high-cocked presumption" (trans. Bowra). This is the traditional interpretation of
the phrase and surely correct, though it has recently been
challenged. The ancient critic Didymos censured Pindar for
his impropriety here and asked, "What reason is there for
Apollo to enjoy the sight of asses in a state of erection?"
Perhaps this is, for Pindar, rather blunt. The sexual theme
will be treated more finely in a later poem, Pythian 9 (to be
discussed in chapter 3). He was only twenty at the time, Farnell says in extenuation, "and the Thessalians would not have
been shocked." One imagines it would have taken a good deal
more to shock those rude Squire Westerns.

The sexual aspect of victory is of course admitted. "The
Greek admiration for physical beauty," Bowra allows rather
blandly, "was all the more powerful because it had a strong

erotic element, and of this of course Pindar was well aware . . ." (*Pindar,* 168). No one denies this but somehow we do not make much of it. Greek poetry has still not been scrubbed quite clean of the decorous neoclassical patina that obscured it for so long, and the effects of centuries of cloistered, clerical study are even more obstructive—that minute, laborious philological labor but for which we could not read the Greek poets at all and which has yet done so much to neutralize the inestimable gift it brought us. Hence even today we tend to blink the fact that those young men who competed naked under the Mediterranean sun must have aroused more than athletic admiration, and that the victor back home must have been the cause of much sexual commotion. Let Pindar speak:

> What a shout as he walked round the ring!
> He was young and beautiful and very beautiful the
>   things that he did.

ὡραῖος ἐὼν καὶ καλός, κάλλιστά τε ῥέξαις (Olympian 9.94). This is not simply praise. The words are gentle as a caress.

The strong sensual excitement in the odes is however only one aspect of a larger excitement, an intensity of feeling that is present almost everywhere. And victory, however much desired, is not a bride; the "embrace of victory" has to be metaphorical. But a metaphor for what? For something that would otherwise not be fully expressible, the astounding joy which Pindar found in these celebrations and which his task was to recreate and make permanent by his tripartite art— words, music, dance—an art that fits the voice of festal splendor to the Doric sandal. There may be an analogue to what Pindar is doing here in the Christian mystics, unlikely though this may appear. Having to express the otherwise inexpres-

sible felicity of union with the divine, the mystics will draw
on the most intense form of earthly experience known to us,
the sexual, and use explicitly even grossly erotic terms to
describe a joy for which there are no direct words, the *fruitio
Dei.* These Greek victors, as Pindar saw them, in the hour of
their triumph (flaming with the clamor of the Graces) and
later during its celebration at home, tasted a joy beyond any
normally granted us, a condition that for a brief space trembles on the border of divinity itself, and yet does so without
the dangers, the sinfulness, that in Greek eyes darkened the
drive to transcendence. What Nietzsche called "the highest
and most illustrious human joys, in which existence celebrates its own transfiguration" (*The Will to Power*, sec. 1051):
here is the burden of the odes, their deepest matter, and what
makes them really difficult. For they come up against a long-
standing, deeply rooted prejudice, in its older, nobler form
the conviction that the supreme vision is the tragic, more recently the sense that literature's proper subject is suffering.
There is no arguing with these beliefs. At the most, one may
ask why joy should not be allowed to express itself as richly
in poetry as it does in music. Certainly it does so less often.
All the more reason to cherish the poet who put joy at the
center of his odes and built for it these ceremonies of praise.
"Festal sublimity is a far rarer thing than tragic sublimity,"
C. S. Lewis once wrote. Rarer, and no less valuable.

To enter this strange world we need all the help we can
get. Recent studies of the form of epinician poetry have removed many old barriers to understanding, but they hardly
take us beyond the level of technique. The Pindar who once
seemed so willful and incoherent may have been replaced by

a consummate virtuoso, but has our new grasp of the genre really brought us any closer to Pindar the great poet or given any true substance to that dusty old claim? Wilamowitz' gloomy pronouncement, "His world is quite alien to us," remains as true today as it was sixty years ago. Or would be so, had not help come from an unsuspected quarter. For perhaps a new means of access has opened up, though it has hardly been noticed. I can make the point most quickly by means of a personal experience. A few years ago I gave a small seminar on Pindar and in the introductory class read Olympian 7 (admittedly one of the easier poems), presenting it with a minimum of technicalities and trying so far as possible to let the text speak for itself. At the end of the class someone said, "But why is Pindar supposed to be so difficult?" The person who asked this question was a poet and familiar with the poetry of this century and found that she could take more or less in her stride things which so puzzled earlier readers—the rapid cutting from one theme to another, the ellipses and apparent lack of connections, the brilliant images imbedded in some pretty impenetrable stuff. Recalling this occasion I find myself wondering about the way a Pindaric scholar, Mary R. Lefkowitz, introduced the poet to beginners in her book *The Victory Ode* (1976). One of the poems she chose was Olympian 1. We had better have the opening lines in front of us; again, I quote the Nisetich translation to show that I am playing fair:

> Water is preeminent and gold, like a fire
>   burning in the night, outshines
> all possessions that magnify men's pride.
>   But if, my soul, you yearn
>   to celebrate great games,
>   look no further

> for any other star
> shining through the deserted ether
> brighter than the sun, or for a contest
> mightier than Olympia—

Professor Lefkowitz examined the opening of the poem carefully and then paused to say this: "As modern readers, rather
than ancient listeners, it is only natural that we might feel at
this point rather dazed. So much has been suggested in so
few words, so many ideas associated that in ordinary life have
no logical relation." The ancient audience, Lefkowitz explained, "more accustomed than we to making connections
between similar words and actions on first hearing, would
have more readily understood the juxtaposition of absolutes
in the ode's opening lines"(p. 82). That is, water, gold, sun,
Olympian games, all supreme in their own sphere. There are
of course different kinds of modern reader. The one I have in
mind is a quick-witted person, not perhaps very well in-
structed but curious and clever enough to get hold of the
information he may lack, and quite at home with abrupt juxtapositions and the association of logically unrelated ideas.
They are after all part of modern life; our jokes and films are
full of them. My modern reader cut his critical teeth on a
poem in which someone walking down a London street meets
a man called Stetson and exclaims "You who were with me
in the ships at Mylae!" and then asks if the corpse he planted
in his garden has sprouted. Such a reader is not notably dazed
by the opening of Pound's fourth canto:

> Palace in smoky light,
> Troy but a heap of smouldering boundary stones,
> ANAXIFORMINGES! Aurunculeia!
> Hear me. Cadmus of Golden Prows!

There are four elements here which Pound juxtaposes, leaving us to work out the relation between them. A ruined city, Troy. The poem has much to say about the rise and fall of cities and the reader has already met Helen *heleptolis,* "destroyer of cities," destroyer of a city called Troy, in the second canto. Next, a sonorous epithet—from Pindar, as it happens: *anaxiforminges,* "[songs] that rule the lyre." It is poetry that told us, long before archaeology, of Troy's fall. Third, Aurunculeia, the name of the bride in a radiant marriage poem by Catullus, representing perhaps (at this stage the reader is simply keeping open a number of possibilities) the creative aspect of sexuality, in contrast to Helen's destructiveness. Fourth, Cadmus, who sailed in pursuit of his abducted sister Europa and founded a new city, Thebes. (Like Menelaos, who sailed in pursuit of abducted Helen; unlike Menelaos, who helped to destroy an old city.) The person quick enough to handle this sort of thing—such people do happily exist—is not, it seems to me, going to make heavy weather of Pindar's illogical associations and compressions and juxtapositions. Far from feeling "rather dazed" by them, he is likely to find himself agreeably challenged and I can imagine him saying, "Hmm, might be this fellow Pindar is worth looking into."

One must be quite clear about the kind and the limits of the help which modern (more properly, modernist) poetry could provide: it could take the reader past the initial obstacles which have caused so much trouble. Then of course he comes up against the differences. The parts of a Pindaric ode are very firmly connected whereas in much twentieth-century poetry the connections may really be missing, suppressed as a matter of poetic strategy. Moreover, Pindar's choral lyric, however much he may have reshaped what he inherited, is a traditional form whose procedures were broadly familiar, while the modern poem aims, in a desperate wager against total noncommunication, to be each time new, spun afresh from its own inner necessities. The similarities, it may be said, are all of the surface. Perhaps so, but they are enough to allow the initial all-important encounter to take place, that first shock of poetic excitement which later study can modify and deepen but never replace. And this can happen without the dulling interposition of learned commentary. Contact once established, the reader can go on to mug up the doctrine of the matter. But he has got the sequence right. It is better, Eliot once said, "to be spurred to acquire the scholarship because you enjoy the poetry, than to suppose that you enjoy the poetry because you have acquired the scholarship."

The surface similarities, though apparently offering only a fragile bridge to Pindar, may however be buttressed by something more solid. There may be a real if remote kinship. Consider a passage like this, a description of medieval Welsh poetry which a critic cites for the light it throws on another great if still too little read modernist poem, *The Anathemata* of David Jones:

> The absence of a centred design, of an architectural quality, is not a weakness in old Welsh poetry, but results quite reasonably from a specific view of composition. English and most Western European creative activity has been conditioned by the inheritance from Greece and Rome of the notion of a central point of interest in a poem, a picture or a play, a nodal region to which everything leads and upon which everything depends. The dispersed nature of the thematic splintering of Welsh poetry is not due to a failure to follow this classical convention. [Welsh poets] were not trying to write poems that would read like Greek temples or even Gothic cathedrals but, rather, like stone circles or the contour-following

rings of the forts from which they fought, with hidden
ways slipping from one ring to another. (Gwyn Williams,
The Burning Tree [1956], 15)

Does not the structural principle in the last sentence (adopted
by David Jones in his poem) sound curiously like Pindaric
ring-composition? More important, the concept of a centered
design, inherited as the writer says from Greece and Rome,
is absent not only in Jones's poem: it is absent in Pindar too.
It is a *classical* concept, informing a classical masterpiece like
the *Oedipus Rex*. Pindar's art, however, is not in this sense
classical; it belongs to an earlier world which we have rather
recently come to call *archaic*. Since this is a large topic, let me
take a single example, the way the archaic writer can move
backwards and forwards in time without regard to chronological sequence. This was a stumbling block to older Pindaric
scholars. Farnell, for example, says of the myth in Nemean 3
that the poet "shows more than his usual carelessness in respect to the order of events." Pindar is telling how the centaur
Kheiron educated Achilles and suddenly "breaks into" this
account with a detail about Kheiron's tutelage of another
hero, Jason, who belonged to an earlier generation. And yet
Pindar seems to put them both on the same temporal plane.
He does this sort of thing constantly, often in far more startling ways. Pound and Jones in our day do precisely the same
thing. In canto 2, I said, Pound introduces the figure of Helen
"destroyer of cities." But look again. It is not Helen who is
thus characterized but Eleanor, patroness of troubadour poets
in the twelfth century A.D. Pound then goes on—trusting in
our ability to make connections between similar-sounding
words and names—to relate what Homer, in the eighth century B.C., said about . . . Eleanor.

The disregard of chronological sequence in the modernist

masters is part of something larger, something that might
open up a directer path to Pindar than any we have had
before. The recovery of the archaic, the new feeling in the art
and thought of our time for archaic images and structures and
modes of thought, has given us access to older, half lost
(sometimes wholly lost) worlds, very much including the
world of pre-Platonic Greece. Again, a single example must
suffice to suggest the kind of kinship we might in consequence enjoy with Pindar. He has a strange and beautiful way
of seeing the city as a living, growing thing. The same conception is found already in Hesiod—"Where the city flour-
ishes, the people flower" (*Works and Days*, 227)—but Pindar
greatly develops it. The Pindaric city is (like?) a tree. Its roots
are the ancestral heroes and their foundational acts, the visible
tree is the city's continuing life, its leaves and flowers the
city's sons and their achievements. The poet's song waters
the roots of the city-tree and ensures that it will continue to
bear its heroic blossom. This organic, vegetal conception of
the human community finds its richest expression in the great
seventh Olympian (the poem which made my admirable student wonder why people found Pindar difficult). The poem
was written for an athlete from Rhodes and the myth presents
three scenes from the legendary history of the island. These
scenes are set in receding chronological sequence ("in his
pleasant wayward fashion," says Farnell, Pindar "reverses the
time-order of events in his mythic world"), each involving an
offense or error, in diminishing order of gravity. Only the
third scene need concern us here. It takes place in the primal
days when Zeus and the other immortals were portioning out
the world between them and "Rhodes was not yet visible on
the sea's face. The island lay hidden in the salt deeps." It
somehow happened that Helios, the Sun, was not present

when the lots were cast and thus received no portion. Zeus then proposed another cast but Helios would not have it:

> For he said that within the grey water
> he saw, burgeoning from the bed
> a land very fertile for men and a friend to flocks.

Helios asked that this land, about to lift into the brilliant air, should be his. The gods agreed. And then the island emerged, grew, from the water. In translation we had better say *rose*, for Pindar takes advantage of the fact that in Greek *Rhodos*, Rhodes, is indistinguishable, in the oblique cases which he uses, from *rhodon*, rose:

> From the salt sea
>   an island rose
> growing into the light! It is his, the Lord
> of Horses whose breath is fire.
> There Helios lay with Rose [Rhodes]
> and fathered seven wiser sons than earlier men
> from his own wit.

Among the issue of these seven were the three men who founded and named after them the three principal cities into which historical Rhodes was divided.

At the start of this chapter I quoted Pound expressing his dislike of Pindar, but the Pindar he disliked was the creature of an old misreading. Had he been able to see through to the true Pindar he would have found in him a friend and a master. For Pound too saw the city as a living, growing thing. In the first canto we are shown, mysteriously, through a jumble of fragmentary quotations (the full vision lies far ahead) Aphrodite emerging from the welter of the sea with her crown of city walls—Aphrodite, Love, Amor. The poem presents a se-

ries of attempts to build the city, the true city where we "political beings" are at home, not the feverish travesty we
endure today. Only much later do we see the process by
which the city comes into being. It grows like a tree:

> The roots go down to the river's edge
> and the hidden city moves upward
> white ivory under the bark.   (Canto 83)

The tree, earliest form of the column; the column that sustains
the temple; the temple that stands at the center of the city.
Pound puts it more simply, in a pun, in the previous canto:
"Let the herbs rise in April abundant." It is a vision very close
to Pindar's, but of the two Pound's is the more archaic.

Let me not be misunderstood. I am not saying that Pindar
is really quite modern after all. He is nothing of the sort. His
poetry is very distant and this distance must be preserved
and cherished. For it is not a void, not an obstacle to be overcome, but rather what Gadamer calls a productive distance
which, while it separates us from Pindar, can also bring us
close to him if we allow it to do so. For this distance is our
tradition, a tradition which, however fractured it may be and
however lightly Pindar belonged to it, still has some hold on
us, can still address us, even when we think to reject it. And
we in our turn can address it and establish a relation to what
it holds, a relation in which both parties have their rights. We
cannot, that is, remove an old work from its time and require
it to take up residence here and show its relevance to us. That
is a mere vulgarization and laying waste of the past. Nor can
we deny our location in the present and transplant ourselves
there. That is the naive error of historicism; the most learned
among us would cut a very poor figure in fifth-century
Thebes. To establish a true relation with a work from the past
is to enter into a dialogue with it. The dialogue may first be

prompted by curiosity or by chance; or by a sense of need, the sense of something there which is missing here and which we want. Something which has cropped up fragmentarily in the art and thought of our time, in answer to an unspoken need of our time, may exist there more richly. It may perhaps be found in Pindar.

One way and another it looks like a good time to turn to this poet who has said so little for so long. Let us make the attempt.

II A POET AND
HIS PACES

Isthmian 6: The Poem as Libation

IN THE SPRING OF 480 B.C., PERHAPS, AN AIGINETAN BOY
called Phylakidas was victor in the *pankration* at the Isthmian
games, held every other year in honor of Poseidon near the
eastern end of the Isthmus of Corinth. A singularly brutal
affair, to our minds, the pankration was a combination of
boxing and wrestling which allowed you to half strangle your
opponent, kick him in the belly or dislocate his limbs. Pindar
was commissioned, no doubt by the boy's father, Lampon, to
compose the poem celebrating this victory. Some time would
elapse before the actual performance, but let us imagine that
the several weeks of rehearsal have been completed, conducted by the poet himself or, in his absence, by a local chorus
master, and that the great day has finally come. The audience
knows in general what to expect from a victory ode and is
eager to see how the poet will ring the changes on the elements required by convention, what novel twists he will introduce. They do not know how the ode will begin—gaily
perhaps or grandly, with some fine moral saying or a glitter
of festive imagery. Much depends on the prelude and Pindar
seldom fails here. The prelude to today's poem is certainly
festive enough; in a way that we will find typical of Pindar it
is richly decorated, intricate, and also extremely neat:

As, the carousal swelling to its height—
"A toast!" so with this second bowl of song
the Muses' draft I pledge
                          Lampon and his athlete sons.
First at Neméa, Zeus, they won your crown of crowns.
Now at the Isthmus
                          Poseidon and the fifty Nereids
garland the youngest son
                    Victor today!
                    Phylákidas!
                          May it be mine to blend
a third grace-offering of delectable song
for Savior Zeus, Olympian, and pour it
here on Aigína's soil.

Three victories: a victory in the Nemean games won by the
young hero's elder brother a year or so ago, his own present
Isthmian victory, and the hope of a future Olympian victory.
It was conventional to pray for this supreme achievement at
the celebration of success in the lesser though still glorious
games. Pindar lays this trio by the side of another, the three
libations or grace-offerings poured on the ground after dinner
to prepare the way, on convivial evenings, for the symposion
("carousal"): the first libation was made to Olympian Zeus,
the second usually to the Heroes and Earth, the third to Savior
Zeus. The simile tries for no mechanical match; tenor and
vehicle preserve their rights while blending harmoniously. By
the end of the stanza we notice that the simile has moved
closer to metaphor as the song becomes a libation poured over
Aigina. The poet is obviously enjoying himself, but not at the
cost of his epinician duties; several required elements have
been smoothly worked in. The victor's father, Lampon, and
the victor himself have been named, the site of the victory

has been given (with a stately bow to the presiding deity, Poseidon, and his sea maidens, the Nereids), his homeland has been identified, and the poet, offering a bowl of song granted by the Muses—vintage stuff, that is, from the very source of poetry—has guaranteed that the celebrant they have chosen will prove worthy of the occasion. Reading the odes as we have recently learned to do, it is hard to remember that Pindar was once thought wayward and undisciplined.

A supremely joyful thing, victory has to be honored; it must also be understood. The poet, that is, must look into its ground and show how it came about. Not certainly by chance, for he goes on in words that are conventional enough but nonetheless thoughtful: "If a man gladly heeding neither cost nor labor builds achievement divinely founded, and if a god plants glory for him. . . ." Another metaphor, as we take "plants" to be, and perhaps we should noti·e here that the first word of the poem in Greek is *thallontos* (metaphorical again, the lexicon tells us), and not knowing quite what to do with it people translate "when the carousal is at its height" or the like. But the verb says: when it is *flourishing*, or *blossoming*. Pindar's is a vegetal world, a world of thrusting energies where things we think of as inanimate or abstract can take on a startling life. We must not pause, though, for the sentence we are looking at, its two conditions satisfied ("if a man . . . , if a god . . ."), is launching into a claim that, although again conventional, can still astonish: "already he casts anchor on joy's farthest shores." It must be the victorious boy Pindar is speaking of, yet he turns at once to his father and tells us of Lampon's prayer that "with thoughts like these he may welcome death and grey old age." A somber, discordant note, to our ears, but the sense of the Greek is rather "May these joyful thoughts last through life." Lampon, in other words, prays for what the poem is striving to bring about: that the brief flash of glory may endure. At the same time, the thought of mortality is here too and serves to set this joy in its human context, within the limited compass of mortal possibility. (To wish for limitless joy—that, to a mind like Pindar's, would be discordant, senseless.) All the more wonderful, then, that beings thus limited should sometimes achieve so much.

The third lobe of the poem's first triad, the epode, finds Pindar still laying the ground plan of his work as he addresses Aigina's ancestral heroes, the Aiakidai, promising to pour his libation of song over them:

> Sons of Aíakos in your golden chariots!
> my surest rule is this, when I come to your island
> to shower you with songs of praise.

Praise of the victor's homeland, another conventional motif, and also another way of looking into the ground or cause of victory, for the blood of the ancestors flows in the veins of every trueborn Aiginetan and it is their bravery in the old days that makes triumphs like the present one possible. This is the central affirmation of Pindar's victory poetry and it prepares the way for the myth he is about to relate. He pauses, as he often does at this point in a victory song, as though in doubt before the sheer abundance of inherited glory he can draw on ("Countless the paths on which your fine acts travel"). Which tale is he to select? "No city so barbarous it has not heard of Peleus," he declares. A myth about Peleus is coming, then, Peleus who married the sea goddess Thetis and fathered Achilles? No, not Peleus, but—emphatically placed at the start of the second triad:

> Aias and his father Télamon.

Aias (Ajax) will figure in the second part of the myth, but

first we are to hear how the Aiakid hero Telamon went with
Herakles on an earlier expedition against Troy, took the city,
slaughtered the Meropes people and killed the giant oxherd
Alkyoneus. Once again the modern reader may find a discordant note and wonder how these bloodthirsty exploits consort with the happy athletic occasion. (They consort well
enough with the brutal reality of the pankration to be sure,
but Pindar never speaks of such matters.) No such thought
would have occurred to the audience. The young men who
are dancing the ode are also trained fighters ready at a moment's notice to take their place in the ranks to defend their
city; the art of dance was not "aesthetic," a category antiquity
was fortunate enough not to possess, but in the Greek sense
political and ministered readily to the art of war. Homer describes a warrior as a dancer, Lucian notes: "His nimbleness
in battle and disciplined movements were gained from dancing." A seventh-century Corinthian wine jug shows a line of
soldiers, their gorgeously decorated shields splayed out like
fans, advancing as though in dance step to engage the enemy
while just behind a kilted piper calls the tune.

Having touched on the highlights of Telamon's career,
the bright speed of the lyric narrative glancing from scene to
scene, Pindar now retraces his steps to the beginning to describe how Herakles first summoned the hero to war. This
way of telling a story used to be taken as a mark of the poet's
muddleheadedness; today it is well understood and perhaps
too much discussed, for ring-composition is a simple enough
attention-catching device. A modern journalist will structure
his story in something of the same way. Herakles, at all
events, turns up and finds Telamon and his companions feast-
ing; Telamon bids him pour the libation, handing him the
magnificent wine bowl "shuddering with gold" which we admired in the previous chapter. The offering of yet another

libation—the poem has already provided us with two or perhaps three—serves to tie the myth to the poem and, beyond
that, to the occasion of the poem, for the simile with which
it opened may well have been designed to dovetail into the
celebration itself (suppose that the performance took place
after a banquet), and at the same time to ennoble that celebration by showing it, in its more modest though still glorious
terms, as the reenactment of something that happened in the
time of the ancestors. The poet now goes on to tie the myth
still more firmly to the poem and its occasion by reaching
down to the foundational event which is the origin or cause
(arkha) of today's triumph. A new energy and excitement
come into the song, the sense of something momentous about
to be revealed, a glimpse granted by victory of the ceremony
and splendor of the heroic age. Herakles, clad in his lion-skin,
prays to Zeus that Telamon may father a son worthy of him:

> "Now, now, at my prayer's urging:
> Grant this man a son and me
> a destined friend in need, lion-strength
> be his unbreakable (the beast's
> pelt rounds me now—I killed him at Neméa,
> my first labor).
> > And heart to match."
> He spoke. And Zeus sent down
> > his eagle, lord of birds.

Gifted now with prophetic powers Herakles declares that a
son will be born to Telamon and that he must be called *Aias*,
after the portent of the eagle (*aietos*), "his people's awe in the
War God's toils." The story ends as it began with the name
of the great Aiakid warrior; the ring has closed on itself.

The relation of myth to ode, though usually far clearer
than an errant critical tradition has made it out to be, is not

often as clear as this. The myth has translated into glowing
narrative terms what the poet earlier stated in bare, discursive
terms. To win the supreme honor of the victor's wreath, we
were told, two conditions have to be met: the victor's achievement must be built on divine foundations, and a god must
plant glory for him. These are in effect two ways of putting
the same thing, two ways of describing the foundational act
by which a god or hero breeds power into a race and from
which all future excellence proceeds. The epiphany of the
eagle heralding the birth of the ancestral hero Aias was a mark
of divine favor granted to the Aiakidai, a favor still at work
in their descendants; it is, more literally than we can imagine,
the cause of Phylakidas' triumph today, the seed from which
it sprang. And as I argued in the first chapter, the process
goes two ways, for present achievement, seconded by the
song which celebrates it, opens a direct path to the foundational event. As the ode is being performed, victor and community, and more distantly we ourselves if we dare to reach
out in imagination to Pindar's world, stand in the sacred light
of the origins. Anthropologists tell us of societies we call primitive which still know such privileged states, but their cultural
reality is too remote to enter with any confidence. Here, and
here alone, a great poet is at hand to mediate the experience
for us.

At this point Pindar indicates that the myth is over and
that he is moving to another theme:

A long business, to spell out the full count of their
glories!

This signal, for that is what it is, is a convention of the genre
which we meet in ode after ode, a structural element belonging to what Bundy calls choral grammar. These signals must
be recognized, but there is no call to make heavy weather of

them or devise ungainly terms for them, let alone treat parts of a poetic form as though they belonged to a piece of machinery.

With this, Pindar returns to the victor and his brother— "these brilliant boys," as he calls them—and their uncle, recounting their various athletic successes. The victory list was an essential feature of the ode, and Pindar can always make it sound grand even when there is not, as apparently here there is not, too much in fact to report. "What a portion of song they have brought up to the light!" he declares impressively, and the words that follow show his pervasive vegetal imagery at work again:

> They nurture their clan
> with the glittering waters of the Graces.

The victors' act, the bestowal of water, recalls and complements the libations we have witnessed, but this is the water of the Graces or Kharites, the divine presences presiding over the epinician occasion who are also spirits of growth and fertility. Victory, consolidated by the poet's song, waters the roots of the family tree. (Hence in the opening words of the poem the carousal was described as "flourishing": it makes things grow.)

The poet next turns once more to the victor's father, Lampon, who plays an unusually prominent role in the poem. He honored and enjoined upon his sons Hesiod's saw—"Practice makes perfect," we might translate—that is, he made them train long and hard, insisting on the sheer slogging perseverance that must come first if divine favor is to crown a man's efforts. Perhaps Pindar saw that, although Lampon may not have been much of an athlete himself, his encouragement was responsible for his sons' prowess. Or perhaps the old gentleman had made clear that his own contribution to the matter was to be given its due weight. We cannot tell. There may well have been some social comedy in the poet's dealings with his clients that is forever hidden from us. Fortunately, since it is the odes that count, and what strikes us is the way Pindar draws everything into the pattern—conventional generic motifs, touches of local imagery sometimes, or seemingly incidental grace notes—and makes them expressive of his theme. The praise of Lampon was required by convention, whether or not there is rather more of it here than we might expect, but note how it is handled. Pindar says of him:

> Measure he pursues in his counsels, yes and achieves
> it.

In the days when Pindar was a preacher—heavy, earnest Pindar as we once, heaven help us, thought of him—this might have been taken as a none too oblique warning to the victor not to let success go to his head. But Pindar is praising not preaching, and measure is the human norm against which Phylakidas' achievement has to be seen. The line thus serves much the same purpose as Lampon's prayer earlier on. Further, perhaps, the words suggest the seemly, traditional world of fine usage from which a true athlete is bred. Pindar was no preacher, but we should not overlook the ethical note in the odes.

The poem ends as it began. The poet began by pledging his hosts in a bowl of song granted by the Muses. He ends with the same gracious gesture (did he raise a cup of wine to his lips as the final words were sung?), but this time the branching associations of the words make the gift richer:

> I will give them a draft of the holy water of Dirka
> which the daughters of Memory golden-robed
> made to spring by the walled city of Kadmos.

The lines take up and put the seal on all the drink-offerings of the poem and make us wonder about their relation. The opening simile of the libation, prompted perhaps by the literal libation ending the banquet before the performance, led to the metaphor whereby the poet's song became a libation poured over Aigina and then over the Aiakidai; this in turn became, in the myth, the literal libation poured from the numinous gold vessel. Then came the metaphorical water with which the sons of Lampon nourished their clan. And here finally is the water proffered by the poet to the family, water drawn from the source of all poetry, the sacral spring which the Muses, daughters of Memory golden-robed, made to spring up. The stately phrase claims attention too, for the Muses' "memory" is both the record of the past but for which we would know nothing of the deeds of the ancestors and at the same time the power which memorializes the fine deeds of the present, makes a memory of them, in Herodotos' phrase, and carries them forward into the future. The water proffered by the poet (that is, the song he has brought with him) is, once again, both figurative and literal: the water of poetry, and the water which the women of his native Thebes carry home every day and which has nourished his bodily frame. Should we distinguish two kinds of drink-offering in the poem, literal and metaphorical? Or does Pindar move so easily between them because for him the distinction is drawn far less sharply? The uses of language which we call metaphorical have been developed to span a rift that has opened up between different kinds of experience. There is much to suggest that for Pindar, who saw the city, like the family, as a growing tree, reality may have been unified to a degree we can imagine only in art (art the augury of restored wholeness, Nietzsche said), so that our distinction between letter and figure hardly holds for him.

His words here have much to say to us, much more than
my translation can suggest, not simply because his are the
words of a great poet but because they speak from a reality
at which we in our riven world can only guess. Let Pindar
then for once address us in his own speech:

πίσω σφε Δίρκας ἁγνὸν ὕ-
   δωρ, τὸ βαθύζωνοι κόραι
χρυσοπέπλου Μναμοσύνας ἀνέτει-
   λαν παρ᾽ εὐτειχέσιν Κάδμου πύλαις.

Olympian 3: The Meaning of Victory

Pindar loved to build from ancestral ground, finding the
origin of the victory to be celebrated in the legendary of the
victor's clan or region. Victors who lacked such a background,
like some of his parvenu overseas clients, forced him to look
elsewhere for what he needed. Thus Olympian 1, composed
for the chariot victory of Hieron, the recently established master of Syracuse, tells the story of the first Olympian chariot
race in heroic time when Pelops defeated Oinomaos and won
his daughter in marriage. Similarly in Olympian 3, reaching
back still farther, Pindar relates the founding of Olympia by
Herakles, even though the victor, Theron lord of Akragas
(modern Agrigento), came of grand mainland stock and
claimed descent from the royal house of Thebes.

The prelude to this ode at once strikes the note of high
solemnity, in the old festive sense of the word, the rich and
stately diction carried on the tide of the sumptuous Doric
cadences telling of the pride of life full-toned and unrepen-
tant. The poet begins by invoking the Twin Horsemen, Kastor
and Polydeukes, patrons of equestrian contest (for this too is
a chariot victory) and tutelary heroes at Olympia, and their

sister Helen. Quickly he proclaims the victor's city and name,
the place of victory and the event in which it was won, then
announces that for this great occasion he has devised "a new
way of fitting the voice of festal splendor to the Dorian sandal"
(some choreographic innovation?). And now our gaze is directed to the proud figure in whose honor the celebration is
taking place:

> For look, that laureled head
> compels me to this God-appointed debt,
> to blend the many voices of the lyre,
> the crying of flutes and disposition of words,
> fitly: for Ainesidámos'
> son. And Olympia too
> calls for my song.

At this point Pindar does something he does nowhere
else (a little later we understand why), presenting in very slow
motion the moment soon after the race when the victor was
crowned. In seventeen exactly paced words we are made to
see the judge, "fulfilling the ancient ordinances of Herakles,"
then a close-up of the victor's eyes, then back to the judge, a
solemn, impartial figure, his raised hand followed by the eyes
which watch it descend to set on the waiting head the

> graysilvered honour of the olive crown.

The action is not yet over, the sentence is still under way,
when suddenly from this very close focus our gaze is led out
to distant time and place. Let us try to watch this happening.
The judge has just placed on the victor's head the

> graysilvered honour of the olive crown, that once
> from Ister's shadowy springs
> Amphítryon's great son
> brought back, best trophy of Olympian contest—

With this, turning on his heel, as it were, the poet does what we will often see him do, glide into the myth on a relative pronoun: a myth about the finding of the tree with whose leaves we have just seen the victor crowned. The sentence is not quite done, but we must leave it at this point to mark the way Pindar fits his material into the formal design of the ode. Olympian 3, like the majority of the odes (37 out of 45), is triadic, composed that is of two matching, metrically equivalent stanzas, strophe and antistrophe (turn and counter-turn, Ben Jonson called them), completed by another stanza, the epode (or stand), with one exception in the same basic meter but patterned slightly differently. The dance movement of the strophe, according to some ancient authorities, was clockwise, that of the antistrophe counterclockwise (vice versa, according to others), while in the epode it seems that the chorus came to a standstill. This triadic sequence, moving through time to build a shape in space, was established by tradition. The material filling the triads, though it too includes many familiar, traditional elements, is obviously different in every poem. Olympian 3 consists of three such triads. The first contains the prelude and ends with the lines I have just quoted. It ends, that is, by introducing the myth, which then fills the whole of the second triad without a break and comes to a close, its energies finally spent, early in the third triad, after which Pindar returns to the victor and his clan and puts the finishing touches to his stately edifice of praise. The ode thus has two structures. There is the formal, triadic design of strophe, antistrophe and epode, upon which the actual content of the poem is laid or against which it is counterpointed. One effect of this double layering must have been to make immediately apparent something that readers confronting Pindar's bare text in the silence of the study have often found so puzzling, the relevance of the myth to praise of the victor

and to the poem as a whole. Since the first triad here devoted
to the victor and the celebration of his victory is metrically the
same as, and presumably to some extent similar in choreog-
raphy to, the second triad containing the myth, the relation
of the two would be visually there before the audience. We
who have not been privileged to experience this great, lost
art form have to reconstruct the relation analytically, but one
thing we can grasp at once: the celebration of this Olympic
victor in the first triad, and his renewed praise in the third,
move to the same tune as the account in the second triad of how
the festival in which he triumphed was originally instituted
and the tree was discovered whose leaves provided the
wreath which we saw placed so deliberately on his head. The
performance of the ode itself establishes a relation between
praise and myth as *fact*. What this fact means (if we decide
that it means anything) is another question and had best be
postponed until we have looked at the myth.

It tells how Herakles (the son of Amphitryon) went to
the land of the Hyperboreans, that fabulous people favored
by Apollo who lived by the banks of the Ister (the Danube)
"beyond the North Wind." There he saw a wonderful grove
of olives, and decided to bring back a cutting to plant by the
racetrack at Olympia. Geographically the Hyperboreans must
reside in the far north, a region unsuited to olives, but myth
does not occupy our geographical space or observe our cli-
mate, and we are not to imagine them residing in some boreal
tract. In Pythian 10 Pindar described them as living in an
earthly paradise untouched by sickness or old age. As one
reads the myth, taking it in the sequence in which Pindar
presents it, no problem arises—provided one allows that
starting at A and going straight through to Z is not the only
way to tell a story. In Isthmian 6 we saw the poet start the
myth at a dramatic point well into the story (Telamon's de-

parture for Troy with Herakles, followed by an account of how
the venture began). Here he starts at the end, at Z:

1. Herakles brought to Olympia from the land of the Hyper-
    boreans the olive tree with whose leaves victors are
    crowned.
2. When (previously) he was laying out the site of the future
    festival and establishing the games, he noticed that no
    trees grew there, leaving the place exposed to the full glare
    of the sun.
3. So he went to the Hyperboreans for trees.
4. He was pursuing a doe with golden horns, a task imposed
    on him by his master Eurystheus through the will of Zeus.
5. While doing so, he saw the trees and marveling at their
    beauty longed to plant them at Olympia.

It is only when we sit back and take pen and paper to this
story (murdering to dissect) that questions arise. A question
about 3: How did Herakles know there were suitable trees in
the land of the Hyperboreans? And about 4: Why did he go
there, to fetch the trees or pursue the doe—or both? A little
reflection shows that Herakles must have made two journeys.
First, the journey in pursuit of the doe, one of his canonical
labors, a familiar story even if the Hyperborean setting is
Pindar's invention. It was on this occasion that he first saw
the trees. Later, when he was founding Olympia, he remembered them and set off a second time. This journey, unlike
the first, was not imposed upon him (line 28) but undertaken,
we are told, at the prompting of his own spirit (25). Pindar,
however, is not much concerned to distinguish the two journeys and in effect combines them or superimposes one upon
the other. It is not too difficult to see why. He wanted a special, wonderful place for the trees to grow in, and he needed
a reason to send Herakles there since the hero's travels were

not (like Solon's later on) inspired by a spirit of philosophical inquiry. An earthly paradise of the sort inhabited by the Hyperboreans was just the place where a tree of the right kind might be expected to flourish—the *elaia kallistephanos,* as it was called, The Olive of the Beautiful Crown, so sacred that the branch with which the victor was crowned could be cut only with a golden sickle by a boy both of whose parents were still living (a perfect youth as yet untouched by the blight of mortality). But how did Herakles come upon this tree? Clearly on one of his labors, and the pursuit of the golden-horned doe was an obvious enough choice since accounts of the regions to which it led him ranged, as a modern mythographer puts it, from the ends of the Peloponnese to the ends of the earth. It was there, then, in pursuit of this fabulous beast in this remote paradise that the tree was revealed to the hero's wondering eyes. In Pindar's usual fashion the finding of the tree encircles the narrative. The conclusion (he brought it back from the Hyperboreans' land) is placed at the end of the first triad just before the start of the myth, the penultimate moment (he longed to plant it at Olympia) near the beginning of the final triad, with the main body of the myth in its customary position, boxed firmly into the central triad. Pindar is tidy about these things.

A good story, then, finely told, with sufficient bearing on its Olympian occasion to justify its presence in the ode. The reward for Theron's victory is a wreath from the tree discovered in ancient days by the greatest of heroes. A sufficient bearing, yes, but Pindar's myths at their best illuminate the fact of victory searchingly, and there may be more to this myth than we have yet seen. In Isthmian 6 the myth culminated with the portent foretelling the birth of Aias, a foundational event which bred into the victor's race the power that gave him his victory. The discovery of the tree in Olympian 3 is not itself foundational in this sense, and only in narrative terms is it the goal to which the myth is driving. Its true subject is the consecration of a holy place. The olive trees are needed to allow this holy place—this garden, Pindar calls it— to fulfill the purpose for which it was appointed: to provide not simply the site, as we would say, but as Greeks said the sanctuary (*alsos*) where, every four years, the Olympic games were solemnly enacted. There may be something in the myth which, while all the time it is addressed to *this* victory, *this* victor (remember the proud, crowned figure watching as the intricate words lift and fall with the song, carried now this way now that by the pattern of the dance), throws light on the nature, the meaning, of victory itself and may thus illu- minate Pindar's epinician poetry as a whole and put to rest a misgiving which sometimes pulls even the seasoned Pin- darist up short: How does the poet contrive to make quite so much of someone winning a race?

Olympia, where Theron's four-horse chariot took the prize (twelve double laps, three accident-prone miles—Greek driving was no doubt as dangerous then as it is now), was not holy because "the games men call holy" were held there. It must have been the other way around. Religious man knows, beyond discussion, that certain places are set apart from others by a special sanctity: *numen inest*. They may be too holy to permit him to set foot there at all, *abata* as the Greeks called them, like the sanctuary of the Eumenides at Kolonos, or they may allow him to enter and establish the appropriate form of worship there. Olympia, where the thun- derbolt of Zeus had fallen and still stood in his precinct, the Altis (as we read in Olympian 10), was such a place. More than half a millennium after Pindar the Greek traveler Pau- sanias wrote that while there are many wonderful things in Greece, "there is a unique divinity of disposition about the mysteries of Eleusis and the games at Olympia" (*Description of Greece*, 5.10.1 [trans. Peter Levi, Penguin Classics, 1971]; more literally, "a special share of God's attention, or care"). If Olympia could still make that impression on a sensitive visitor in the enlightened age of Hadrian, how much stronger must the aura have been in Pindar's day—a place not simply holy but, as German can say, *durchgottet*, engodded through and through. We need not conjecture, however, for Pindar tells us what Olympia was like. The altars of Zeus had already been consecrated, he says, and Herakles "had established the sacred rules for the great games and the Four-Year Rite by the hallowed banks of the Alpheos." Something was missing, though:

> But Pelops' Field did not flower
> fine trees in the valley that lies by Kronos Hill.
> Lacking their shade he saw the garden naked,
> enslaved to the Sun's fierce rays.

The garden, as it was to be, lay exposed to the full unshaded glare of divinity; that is what first marked it off as holy. But the sons of earth may not stand directly open to the *himmlisches Feuer*, as Hölderlin will say. Man cannot sustain the full presence of God; it must be tempered if he is to endure it. This again is exactly what Pindar says, in poetry's way of saying. Immediately before the lines I have just quoted we are shown Olympia in this very different light, bathed in a soft lunar radiance:

> Full upon him at her midmonth the Moon
> kindled from her golden car the rounded eye of
> evening.

If there were trees encircling the course to intercept and temper the fire of heaven, then Olympia would be a place where

mortals might enter and worship. So Herakles goes off to the
ends of the earth in search of some suitable trees.

This much we haltingly understand. We know about or
at least have read about the founding of sacred sites. What
makes the special sanctity of Olympia hard to grasp is the
form of worship practiced there: athletic contests or, more
exactly, *winning* athletic contests. For the Greeks did not, as
the English claim to do, play for the sake of the game; they
fought their games, ruthlessly, for the single purpose of winning. Victory is what Olympia is about: victory, so great a
thing that it brings the victor rewards which Pindar must
strain the full resources of his art to express, while the vanquished are left to crawl home down back alleys in disgrace.
This is what pulls us up short, this blazing affirmation at the
heart of every ode. So, not knowing what to make of it, we
patronize Pindar: a great poet, but strangely limited in his
interests.* Or we remind ourselves that the games were religious ceremonies and that Pindar was a very religious
man—which is no help at all since if religion now means
anything it means something quite different. Or we avoid the
problem altogether by concentrating on epinician form and
technique. And yet Pindar tells us again and again why victory matters so much. In that radiant moment a man stands
on the edge of the absolute, narrow line separating mortal
from god. Absolute, because our brief lives and powers are
as nothing compared with the unending splendor of Olympos. Narrow, because—in the poet's own words—"somehow
we resemble the immortals, in greatness of mind or bodily

---

*"We feel that he takes the games too seriously, and that when Aeschylus
was wrestling with the deep problems of life and death, the day was past
for regarding an Olympian victory as the grandest thing in the world." J. B.
Bury, *A History of Greece* (1900), 307. And yet Bury was one of Pindar's most
sensitive readers.

form" (Nemean 6). If Zeus represents the natural order in all its majesty, we who are part of that order can at fullest stretch put on a little of his majesty. Victory in the great games enacted in this holy place is the means whereby a momentary gleam of divinity is realized through human effort, by that creature who of all things on earth is the least divine, being the most irretrievably mortal. This is the mystery which Pindar knew himself called on to celebrate.

Olympian 14: The Graces

Written perhaps in 488 when Pindar was thirty, Olympian 14 consists of only two twelve-line stanzas. One doesn't know whether to remark, with Gildersleeve, on their "massive structure" or on the singular delicacy of their build and detail. The victor, named Asopikhos, had won the footrace at Olympia. He was apparently still a boy and came from Orkhomenos in Pindar's own province of Boiotia, once "as famous and glorious a city as any in Greece," Pausanias wrote (Description of Greece, 9.34.5), a great center in the Mycenaean period but now fallen on quiet days and renowned only for its cult and sanctuary of the Graces. They were worshipped there in the form of three great stones which were said to have fallen from heaven.

The poem opens tranquilly with an invocation to the indwelling powers that is at the same time a picture of the land they make blessed. Only two details, but they are enough:

> Yours are the waters of our river,
> the meadows our fine horses graze are yours,
> royal ones of song,
> Graces of Orkhómenos the fertile.

The timeless pastoral landscape takes on a temporal dimen-

sion as the poet addresses the Graces as "wardens of the
ancient race of Minyas," the legendary king of Orkhomenos
whose people, the Minyai, sailed on the Argo for the Golden
Fleece and did great things in the elder days. "Listen to my
prayer," he goes on:

> For it is by your gift
> all that is dear to mortals comes to be,
> if a man is wise or beautiful or victory's shine is on
> him.

A comprehensive glance at the services which the Graces perform for mankind, the third line gives a hint that this is an
epinician, for the beauty of the victor, especially a boyish victor, is often singled out for praise, and "wise" is a word commonly used of poets. (I have overtranslated the third epithet,
aglaos, literally "shining," which can simply mean "famous"
but readily suggests the radiance, aigla, surrounding a victor.)
From earth the ode rises to tell of the services which the
Graces perform on Olympos—"Not even the gods marshal
their feasts and dances / without the holy Graces"—providing a hint, if we are looking for it, of the festivities taking
place here at Orkhomenos. Grandly the stanza ends with:

> Their thrones
> are set beside Apollo Golden Bow, and there
> they honor the glory of Zeus, Olympian father, which
> rolls on forever.

The term used of Zeus's glory has often, from the scholiast
on, been dulled to mean simply "everlasting," but we should
keep the literal sense and let this stanza which began with
an earthly river hallowed by the Graces round to its close with
Zeus (the god honored in the Olympian games) whose glory
flows on like a river.

The poem is half over and so far there has been no explicit mention of either victor or victory. Of the various elements
we look for in the opening part of an epinician, only
one has appeared and taken pride of place, praise of the victor's homeland. This is regularly present and indeed required,
but sometimes the victor's person and achievement bulk so
large that it can seem almost one of his attributes, even
though it is there that the poet will seek the origin of that
achievement. Often he must dig for it, so deep that occasion-
ally we are not at first sure how what he has come up with
bears on the occasion. But in this case the land and the powers
which make it holy are so plainly the source of the victory
that all attention can go there.

It would be quite wrong to take this emphasis on one
epinician element as a sign that the poet felt he could make
nothing of the others, and imagine him saying to himself:
"The boy has precious little going for him. No previous victories and I doubt his family has the means to train and enter
him for any more big events, so there goes the prayer for
future victory. His people have no athletic record, not even
an uncle who picked up a pot somewhere. I shall just have
to make do with praise of the homeland and a prayer to the
Graces." This, certainly, would be wide of the mark. And
there is another more sensitive error into which some older
critics fell. Responding to the accent of genuine religious emo-
tion in this ode, Wilamowitz thought that the commission was
no more than the external occasion giving Pindar the oppor-
tunity to put into words his personal devotion to the goddesses. It is this sort of error—as we now take it to be—that
a recent critic has in mind when he says that "the decorative
intention of the prelude" (half the poem at least!) is apparent.
But that is simply a failure of reading. There is every reason
to believe that the Graces meant a great deal to Pindar and

that his devotion to them finds beautiful expression here. To say this, however, is not at all to say that he intruded his private feelings into a poem designed for a public occasion; rather, he saw that he would best serve his young client by letting the Graces take the primary stress. If there had been victory poetry at Assisi the victor would not have felt scanted of the attention he deserved because the poet spent much of his time on a fervent prayer to St. Francis.

So important are these goddesses to all Pindar's poetry and to this poem in particular that it is worthwhile trying to determine what role they play there. The three Graces, or Kharites—Aglaia, Euphrosuna, Thalia: a famous trio, but who exactly are these ladies and what do they do? We have first to clear our minds of their later representations in poetry and art, one rosy-buttocked maiden flanked by two compan- ions *en face*, pretty or merely tinsel remnants of Olympus' faded hierarchy. We must guard too (a more recent tempta- tion) against seeing them simply as epinician conventions and be careful when Bundy tells us that Euphrosuna is "a poetic name for a victory revel." She is, and yet without Euphrosuna and her sisters the revel celebrating victory would be no more than a beano, nor indeed would there be any victory to cel- ebrate. Our typography too causes difficulties, making us distinguish between *kharis* or plural *kharites*, lowercase, sup- posedly meaning "splendor, glory, blessing," and various other things, and capitalized Kharites, bona fide goddesses now, "the Graces." As soon as we take these distinctions to Pindar's poetry they become very hard to draw. Near the opening of Olympian 7 he describes the victor as one on whom Kharis *zōthalmios* looks, as rich and untranslatable a trouvaille as Yeats's "great-rooted blossomer": Kharis (the three goddesses concentrated into one) who makes life blos- som, we might translate, the fostering grace of life. At the end of the same poem it is said that with the kharites of the victor the city too has *thaliai*. Seeing that modern editors here use lowercase, we take the meaning to be that "with the victor's glory the city too has a festa," for whereas Thalia is one of the Graces (uppercase Kharites, that is), thaliai, lowercase and plural, means "festivity." It is hard to put much faith in these discriminations or be confident that what we read on our printed page is what Pindar's auditors heard. In Nemean 4 he says that it is thanks to the Kharites that a poem comes into existence, but sometimes it seems to be more the other way about, for in Nemean 9 it is the poem that makes victory, newly come to flower (*neothalēs*), burgeon. Or is the agent really Thalia, at work in the epithet modifying victory?

If we take our problem to Slater's Pindaric lexicon we find, to summarize a long entry, that kharis is the splendor and glory granted by victory and is also the poem praising the victory; it is the bond of goodwill and gratitude between victor and poet that is sealed by the victory poem, and sometimes that poem itself; it is the divine power of fertility quickening the limbs that won the victory (here I am reaching beyond Slater to other authorities) and inspiring the poet who celebrates it; it is the gladness in which the festivity crowning the victory is bathed; it is the favor or grace granted by a god which makes victory possible in the first place. To us, then, kharis looks like a horrible confusion or a rich and glorious tangle, depending on one's point of view. To Pindar, there was a seamless whole here that he would have thought it ungrateful (ἄχαρις) and probably impious to dissect and analyze. He must quickly have seen—to return to Olympian 14—that here, on their home ground and before their very temple, in this poem for a victor from Orkhomenos, the Graces must play the central role, and that if in a brief space he could convey all that they meant and all they gave, and then bring this concentrated richness to bear on the boy, he would have a victory poem the like of which no victor had ever been granted. In the second, final stanza this is what we see the poet doing.

He begins by again invoking and ceremoniously naming the three goddesses: Aglaia, the splendor or radiance surrounding a victor; Euphrosuna, the joy of victory and its celebration; Thalia, not simply festivity but *floraison*, in the words of Jacqueline Duchemin, "la fête et son allégresse, dans la soudaine et triomphale explosion des forces de vie" (*Pindare: Poète et prophète* [1955], 240).

> Shining One!
> and Joy, lover of song, listen now,
> daughters of heaven's king, and you, dance-delighting
> Flourisher! mark this festal troop
> how lightly they step for the favor befallen us.
>   And hear what I have brought,
> my Lydian tune, my meditated art,
> song for Asópikhos.

Things are starting to happen, with the goddesses now taking a direct part in the proceedings. We should perhaps note, a small delicate stroke, that while the first two are invited merely to listen, it is Thalia, "Flourisher," who is asked to turn her eyes on the group bringing Asopikhos, still a boy and hence in her special care. Across the plain, hitherto empty of human presences, a line of people is moving to the temple by the river, the young victor at their head or in their midst. And stepping out beside them like a festival piper we may imagine the poet, playing his Lydian tune. For unlike the majority of the odes, designed to be danced in some open place in the city, Olympian 14 is what is called a processional and was sung by the celebrants as they advanced to the temple to give thanks or, perhaps more likely (since no one has explained how Pindar's meters, as complex in the procession-als as in the other poems, could be fitted to any steady for-ward movement), the celebrants first made their way to the temple accompanied by music, and sang the ode there in the immediate presence of the goddesses.

All that remains, now that the victor has been named, is to announce his victory. The announcement is made in five proud words, the loudest in the poem, recording as though for an inscription that by grace of Thalia Olympian victory has come to the land of the Minyai.

Here, on this note of festal joy, the poem might end. But there is one person who, though not directly present, must play his part in the occasion, the person who above all others should share in the victor's good fortune: the boy's dead fa-ther. A shadow seems momentarily to fall across the bright scene as the poet bids Echo take the news, the actual sound of the celebration, to him:

> Go now, Echo, to the dark wall
> of Persephone's house with famous news for his father.
> When you see Kleodámos, tell him his boy
> in the fold of Olympia's valley
> with the wings of a proud victory garlanded his young
>   hair.

It is easy to go wrong here. In the original the word order, with "young" and "hair" placed at the end of their lines and widely separated, emphasizes the two words and gives them, I think, a certain poignance. Should we press harder and find a touch of pathos—the young victor, the dead father? Again, are we to stretch these figurative wings until they hold out a hope of immortality (as in the lines of Theognis, which Pindar seems to have known well*): wings to lift the victor above the mortal scene? This is surely here, for it is implicit in every victory ode; yet if it is here it is here only lightly. Who would want to rise far above *this* earth? The thrust of transcendence, the reach for a more or a beyond, would be a false note in this poem which, in Wallace Stevens' phrase, exiles desire for what is not because everything is present, and accepted. The young life lifts for a moment and soars, later, in the proper season or too soon, to fall back into this sanctified earth, as Kleodamos has fallen. The shadow is needed in order to accent—with hardly a hint of pathos—the brightness of the world of the living from which the dead are set apart but not altogether excluded.

Nemean 3: Out of the Strong Came Forth Sweetness

Of the forty-five victory odes that have come down to us, Pindar composed eleven for the island of Aigina, more than for any other place. We have read one already, Isthmian 6, and will be reading others, for they include some of his finest and most interesting work. Since the pan-Hellenic fame he came to enjoy must have allowed him to pick and choose among commissions, one may suppose that some special sense of kinship drew him to Aigina. It is not in fact difficult to see why he should have felt at home on the island and relished the chance of praising the virtues which shone in her athletes. Like his native Thebes, Aigina was an oligarchy, ruled by a small group of powerful families boasting an illus-

---

*"I have given you wings to fly with ease above the boundless sea and every land. . . . And when you go to the wailing in the house of Hades deep in the glooms of earth, even in death you will never lose your fame, but men will take thought of you, an immortal name for always." *The Elegies of Theognis*, lines 237 ff.

trious ancestry and possessing a round share of this world's goods. Set plumb in the middle of the Saronic Gulf, within sight of her persistent maritime rival Athens, Aigina was a great trading center and dispatched her vessels to every part of the Aegean. "Mistress of the Dorian Sea," Pindar called her; "eyesore of the Peiraeus," Pericles preferred to say. And "Aigina of the long oars" distinguished herself no less in war than in commerce. At Salamis her naval contingent was inferior in size only to that of Athens and when the war was over she was judged to have been superior in valor, a verdict that no doubt gave more satisfaction in Aigina than in Athens.

But what must above all have drawn Pindar to Aigina was her wealth of heroic saga, richer even than the legendary of Thebes. Here was just the kind of ancient, rooted community where his genius flourished most happily. The nymph Aigina, sister of his own Theba, had had the supreme honor of becoming the bride of Zeus, and in some strangely romantic lines Pindar tells how the god carried her off and, "as the golden tresses of the air shadowed the mountain ridge of the land that was to be hers, [laid her down] on an immortal bed." (paian 6.132ff.) She bore him Aiakos, the island's tutelary hero, a man so wise that he settled disputes even among the gods. His shrine, the Aiakeion, occupied a prominent position in the city, a square enclosure walled by white stone (as Pausanias describes it for us, *Description of Greece*, 2.29.6) containing an altar to the hero set amid olive trees. Several odes show that victory celebrations might be performed before or even within this holy place. The sons of Aiakos, the Aiakidai, number some of the great names in Greek saga. There was Peleus, who won the sea goddess Thetis in a marriage—Pindar's emblem for the crown of mortal felicity—attended by the Olympians themselves. The fruit of this marriage was the great Achilles, for Pindar always an Aiginetan. Another of

Aiakos' sons, Telamon, as we heard in Isthmian 6, fought by
the side of Herakles in the first campaign against Troy and
fathered the great war-man Aias who ruled over nearby Salamis. Again and again in the Aiginetan odes Pindar digs
down into this rich loam, finding there the seed or origin of
the virtues that flowered anew in the athletic triumphs of the
island's latest sons.

We would give a lot to know what life was like in this
interesting community, know it in the way we can know what
went on in Venice during the great centuries, but this is the
kind of knowledge time has denied us and we must be content
with the reflection of that life caught in the poet's stately
phrases. A pair of epithets he employs in the seventh Nemean
may point to something that, in his eyes, characterized the
place, a blend of sweetness and violence. Let the poet speak
in his own voice:

> πόλιν γὰρ φιλόμολπον οἰκεῖ δοριϰτύπων
> Αἰαϰιδᾶν.

The victor lives in a city that is *philomolpos*, one which loves
the *molpē*, that combination of music and dancing which is at
the heart of choral lyric. Aigina, then, was an artistic place,
as we would say, where music and dancing and poetry were
eagerly cultivated; they were exacting judges of epinician
verse there. That is one side of the coin. It was also a warlike
place, home of the *doriktupoi* sons of Aiakos, "spear-clashers"
whose martial virtues lived on in their descendants, men
quick to arm and practiced in battle. Aigina, city of dancing
killers.

I am not suggesting that this contrast is peculiar to the
Aiginetan odes, though perhaps it is particularly clear there;
it is something we constantly come up against in Pindar. The
epinician ode celebrates a victory in the games which, how-

ever brutal the actual contest may sometimes have been, belonged preeminently to the arts of peace. For the duration of
the greatest of the games, the Olympian, the warring Greek
states observed a sacred truce. In order to lay bare the origin
of the victories he celebrates, Pindar looks to the past and
normally finds what he is after in the actions of a hero—
violent, even murderous actions as often as not. Take the third
Nemean ode. The main myth begins with some warlike en-
terprises of the earlier generation of Aiakidai; it turns next to
Achilles, showing him first as a boy hunter killing wild beasts,
then, fully grown, doing great things at Troy. The story ends
with a killing which seems especially to have impressed Pindar, the death at Achilles' hands of Memnon, son of the dawn
goddess. Framing this turbulence is a description of the
chorus at the beginning of the ode as "craftsmen of the honey-
toned revel" and, near the end, a comparison of the ode to a
potion composed of milk and honey. *And, behold, there was a
swarm of bees in the carcase of the lion.*

The prelude to Nemean 3, written for a victor in the pankration, one Aristokleidas, is strikingly original. At the start
of an ode Pindar will often give us a phrase or so descriptive
of the occasion. He does that here but he also does something
odder, calling on the Muse to bring into existence the poem
that has already begun and to grant him the words, a gift that
the words we are listening to testify has already been granted.
The effect is to fuse two discrete moments, the poem's genesis
and its composition. And a third is added, its realization in
performance: "Come to this Dorian island of Aigina," he bids
the Muse, "for by the waters of the Asopos the young men
are waiting"—and there follows the vividly sensuous phrase
about the craftsmen of the revel which allows us to imagine

what a Pindaric ode actually sounded like. "They seek your
voice," he goes on:

> Different actions thirst for different things.
> Victory in the games loves song most of all.

Their desire for the Muse's voice, here rephrased thematically,
expresses the bond between word and act governing every
epinician ode. They belong together, neither is complete without the other. The act has ontological priority but can achieve
the permanence it longs for only if it is consummated by the
praising word. The word gives the act a longer life, thereby
winning for itself something of the permanence which it too
longs for but can enjoy only if the act first grants its reason
for being.

Another, more stately call to the Muse ("Begin, then,
daughter of heaven's lord in the deep cloud, sing for him an
acceptable song"), and two more aspects of the performance:
"I will entrust the song to the young men's voices and to the
lyre," the lyre which the poet himself, standing in their midst
(in reality, why does it always have to be by convention?), is
playing. The song, he goes on, "will have a graceful labor,
the glory of the land where of old the Myrmidons [earliest
inhabitants of Aigina] lived, whose famous piazza Aristokleidas did not shame by thews gone slack in the burly ranks of
the pankration." The language needs watching here, for the
word translated glory (or perhaps, glorification), *agalma*, can
also mean a statue, and the word for labor (*ponos*) may also
mean that which labor produces, an artifact. The song which
glorifies the land, then, also creates or becomes, momentarily,
a statue, a statue imagined as standing in the famous piazza
(where the Aiakeion was situated, we suppose). So the place
of the ode's performance has now been identified. And the
durée desired by the act is already being granted. But only

momentarily, for the victor is at once returned to the dust and heat of mortal existence, to "Nemea's deep-lying meadow where he won a balm to heal the blows that wore him: victory song." And now, all the essential preliminaries of the poet's commission having been worked in (except for the name of the victor's father, to be given immediately), now for the soaring claim required by epinician convention that Aristokleidas has touched the summit of human achievement, what Bundy calls the categorical vaunt. It takes the ne plus ultra form we soon come to expect:

> Though he is comely and his acts accord with his
>   beauty,
> this son of Aristóphanes, who has gone
> to the top of man's endeavour, hard it is
> to reach out on untracked water
>   past the pillars
>
> the hero god set up for famous seamark
> of furthest sail.

The sense, as usual in Pindar, is Look how far he has gone!— rather than Let him go no further!—even if our ears instinctively detect a note of warning. Dante's Ulysses, coming to these pillars established "acciò che l'uom più oltre non si metta," does what "Faustian" man must do, presses disastrously, gloriously, on into the forbidden region. The temptation to transgress against limit is not simply later Western, as Spengler thought; it is Greek, or rather Athenian. The Sophoclean hero is so tempted and must be cautioned against thinking more than mortal thoughts. How little the Pindaric hero is tempted is shown in the lines that follow where we watch the hero-god himself, Herakles, on his mission of civilization, slaying monsters and exploring earth and sea until he comes to the straits that close the Mediterranean. There, faced with the limitless ocean ahead, "the darkness beyond Cadiz," as Pindar puts it elsewhere, he at once turns back. In the poet's words, "he reached the bounds that sent him home."

Herakles' exploits, though they look as if they are forming the matter of the myth, prove to be only heroic ornamentation enlivening the ne plus ultra topos, for after a few lines the poet breaks off ("Heart, to what foreign cape / do you bend your course awry?") and bids himself seek his theme "at home," in some Aiginetan tale of Aiakos and his sons. The effect is to pay a graceful compliment to his hosts; their legendary is so entrancing, "matter for sweet utterance," the poet calls it, that even the greatest of heroes must give way to them. The myth which follows, Aiakids going great guns as ever, calls for no special comment. It is handsomely told and tied firmly to the victor by a gnomic statement between its two main sections (deeds of the earlier Aiakidai, youth and manhood of Achilles): "There's a weight of inherited glory in the race." Beginning near the middle of the second triad, the myth fills the third and comes to a strong close with the killing of Memnon. The concluding triad, riding the crest of the excitement that has been generated, opens triumphantly with

Beacon of Aíakid light far-flames afield from there!

"From there," that is, from the Trojan War. Though it is not explicitly stated, we are aware of the usual two-way movement: the old bravery is the cause of the contemporary triumph which in turn makes present again the bravery of the old days. As we come to expect at this stage of an ode, familiar epinician elements now make their appearance—a prayer to Zeus for whom the Nemean games were performed (Zeus who fathered Aigina's heroic line), and another burst of praise for the victor. Conventions of the genre, as we must call them, and yet, such is Pindar's art, each time seeming freshly coined:

> Yours is the blood, O Zeus, yours the contest that my
>   song targets
> as the young voices chant their country's joy.
> Clamor of victory best suits Aristokleídas!
> He has joined this island to fair report.

Here, conventionally again, our excitement is contained by some reflective lines setting today's achievement in the light of traditional lore. Each of life's three stages has its special virtue and activity, the wise poet tells us, perhaps with Hesiod's tripartite division in mind: "Deeds for the young, counsels for the middle-aged, prayers for the old" (fragment 321, ed. Merkelbach and West). There is in addition a fourth virtue, applying to every age: "Heed the here-at-hand." A constant of Pindar's ethical doctrine—do not fix your gaze on distant things, he says in the third Pythian: "Know what lies to hand and what is granted us"—the passage restates in abstract terms the exemplary wisdom of Herakles' refusal to go beyond the pillars (and the poet's in cutting short the story of Herakles and seeking his theme at home). Here, though, the admonitory tone may be uppermost; no doubt these triumphant young men could do with a steadying reminder that tomorrow they must step down from their dizzy pinnacle and rejoin the community.

The poem's business is nearly done and the poet, saluting the victor ("Hail, my friend"), presents a potation composed, by the usual account, of milk and honey capped by the foam of their blending. Since this is known to be something that Greeks did drink, the poet may be offering the mixture in lieu of the cup of wine with which he sometimes

toasts the victor. Milk and honey, however, do not produce
foam, as Gilbert Norwood discovered when he once tried mix-
ing them, and he therefore proposed that the word usually
thus translated (*eersa*) means not foam but water, as it does
at Nemean 7.79 (*Pindar* [1945], 267). If so, there are not two
ingredients but three, and the draft is not a drink presented
to the victor but a libation offered for him and made to the
presiding Muse, invoked at the beginning of the poem and
again a few lines later. However this may be, it is more important to notice that what Pindar is presenting,

> a cup of song carried on the breath of Aeolian flutes,

is less an actual drink than a poetic emblem, like the "reso-
nantly embroidered headband" of Nemean 8 or the garland
we will hear about in Nemean 7, composed of ivory, gold,
and sea flower. Notable too, to pick up my earlier point, is
the fact that this poem, loud with the violent doings of the
Aiakidai ("matter for sweet utterance," the poet called them),
should be compared to so dulcet a potion. What immediately
follows insists on the contrast still more strongly:

> It is late, yes. But the eagle is a quick bird.
> Searches, swoops from high, and
>   suddenly
> the bleeding prey's in its claws.

The song issuing from the honey-toned voices and likened a
moment ago to the honeyed drink-offering has now by another figure become this bleeding thing held in the eagle's
talons. Sweetness and violence indeed.

   Why are we told, rather emphatically (the words telling
us so open the final epode), that the poem is late? From the
scholiast's time until yesterday the answer was taken to be
simply that it was late. The idea of Pindar as "a delinquent

fulfiller of commissions" has however not commended itself
to recent scholarship and it is now being argued that the
poem's lateness is "internal," a ploy to heighten the pleasure
of the return to and renewed praise of the victor in the final
triad after the Mediterranean-wide search for the sources of
his triumph in the preceding triads. This may be so; there is
no way of proving that it is not, but we need feel under no
compulsion to accept the new reading. Commissions were
after all very much part of an epinician poet's life and the
poem may in fact have arrived a few weeks late; even a great
epinician poet must sometimes have missed a deadline.
"Love's not so pure, and abstract, as they use / To say, which
have no Mistresse but their Muse," Donne wrote. Perhaps
Pindar's odes are not so pure and abstract as critics suppose
who, overreacting against the historical, biographical researches of Wilamowitz, have burned too much midnight oil
over Bundy's epinician grammar. Allow that the poem really
was late and observe how skillfully Pindar turns a potential
source of embarrassment to his credit. By the figure of the
eagle he banishes all thought of any possible remissness, di-
recting our attention instead to the imperious speed with
which he serves his patron. A bold procedure, a little bare-
faced perhaps and surely not a little witty. And more than
that; the lines embody a key epinician theme. At the start of
the ode we had the young men searching (*maiomenoi*) for the
Muse's voice; here at the close is the eagle searching after his
prey (*metamaiomenos*, a compound of the same verb) and
swiftly taking hold of it. The act seeks the word, the word
seeks the act and, finally, the complete consort dancing together, they are joined to each other.

The poem is over. No, not quite, the victory list is still to
come. It comes, at the very end, in a single commanding
sentence:

From Neméa, from Epidauros, from Mégara,
                                    the light   has   looked.

○ ○ ○

It is salutary sometimes, after spending enough time on
a poem of Pindar's for its intricate manoeuvres to come to
seem familiar, to stand back and let it confront us again as
something strange and alien. What impression does this
poem make if we stand back from it, this song of praise for a
comely young victor in the pankration who acted in a manner
befitting his beauty, kicking his opponent in the belly, perhaps, half strangling him or wrenching his foot out of its
socket, and then some time later received his reward, a poem
as elaborately beautiful as a Bach fugue, performed by the
honey-toned craftsmen of the rites of revel celebrating the
turbulent powers of their race come to flower again in this
young hero of the hour?

The contrast between sweetness and violence, the sweetness of the danced poem in praise of victory, the violence
which gained the victory and is seen by the poet as its ground:
this may no doubt cause surprise but it ceases to do so if we
once let our minds range back in time. For most of our history,
violence and great art—high culture in general—have gone
together happily enough. Only for the last century or so and
then only for the more privileged classes of Western Europe
and North America has life not been lived at close quarters
with violence, and now it is everywhere returning. "We have
lit upon the gentle, sensitive mind / And lost the old nonchalance of the hand," Yeats wrote before our century showed
itself in its true colors. Perhaps the hand's old nonchalance,
the artist's hand as well as that of the man of action, fails
when the mind grows too gentle. The sensitive mind may

prompt social reform. There is nothing to suggest that it creates high culture.

What should fruitfully perplex us is rather the picture of Herakles at the pillars ("the bounds that sent him home"), proposed by the poet as exemplary and enforced by the injunction to heed what lies to hand and not venture beyond the mark. Our minds are so constituted that we must think this no way for a hero to behave. What sort of hero is it who comes to the dangerous edge of things and then simply turns back—as though bounced off the sides of some cosmic billiard table? Can questing man at a certain point give up his quest and retreat? And surely heeding (only) what lies to hand must fatally stunt our power of reach? This Nemean ode, if we contrive to station ourselves before it in such a way that it can address us, challenges us here, posing a question or choice that is starting to take shape. George Steiner points to it at the end of his essay *In Bluebeard's Castle* (1971) when he speaks of "the conviction centrally woven into the Western temper, at least since Athens, that mental enquiry must move forward, that such motion is natural and meritorious in itself" (p. 136). We will open the last door of Bluebeard's castle even if (perhaps *because*, Steiner suggests) it gives on to realities wholly beyond our control. More than ever this is now the Western way. There are or have been other ways, of course, the way for instance of those primitive societies which "have chosen stasis or mythological circularity over forward motion, and have endured around truths immemorially posited." To put the choice in these terms is to leave us no choice: better advance, however perilous or disastrous, than stasis, the indignity of vegetable repose. But the terms Steiner uses are, inevitably, ours, not Pindar's. The world of his poetry, in no sense a primitive one, is greatly energetic; it is at the same time, in the most literal sense, limited and chooses to endure round its immemorial truths rather than advance. The ne plus ultra of those limitary pillars, which we see as restrictive, is for him constructive, a grace of containment providing man's energetic nature with the space within which it can flourish in the manner that is proper to it. Words that we hear as admonitory and even craven proudly affirm that saving grace. It may be too late to hear those words as Pindar speaks them.

III INTERLUDE: AN ODE TAKES SHAPE (NEMEAN 10)

In his long career as epinician poet pindar faced the same problem again and again. So and so had won such and such a contest and must be praised in a way that made the victor in a footrace or wrestling match seem to stand at the top of human achievement. Pindar could not of course have written as he did without his belief in what one may call the meaning of victory. He was helped too by something that to most poets since the Romantic movement would look more like a handicap, the strict conventions governing his genre which saved him from having to strain for ever more extravagant flights of hyperbole in the manner of baroque panegyric. The problem was nonetheless formidable and the wonder is that he tackled it with such unflagging energy and wealth of fresh invention. Every ode resembles, must resemble, every other in many ways and yet each possesses its special flavor and tone, so that to say Pythian 9, Nemean 8, Pythian 8, is to conjure up three quite distinct poetic landscapes.

I want for once to try to trace in imagination the genesis of an ode—not the mysterious process whereby a work of art comes into being, but the way a writer observing strict conventions and with a patron to satisfy goes about his task. The attempt to peer into the poet's workshop cannot be more than speculation, yet it may throw light on things that a more formal analysis does not tidily handle. Take the ode known as Nemean 10—wrongly, since it commemorates not a Nemean

victory but one gained in the festival of Hera at Argos. An
Argive called Theaios had won the wrestling match there and
commissioned Pindar to write the celebratory song. Argos, an
ancient city as rich in myth and heroic legend as the poet's
own Thebes, was the sort of place where Pindar felt at home.
He may have been there before; let us suppose that he revisits
it to refresh his memories. He spends several days simply
strolling through the streets and squares, letting impressions
come over him as they will and soaking up the atmosphere
as he looks for the ground from which this victory grew.
Everywhere he comes across memorials to the great past and
witnesses to the timeless—fine new work in bronze and, even
more to his taste, ancient things which, though the crafts-
manship might seem rude by the refined standards of the day,
are full of god. On his way to Argos he had stopped a few
miles out of Mykenai at the great sanctuary of Hera, goddess
of the city, and prayed before her wooden image. Learning
his name, a priest had pointed out an altar showing the marriage of Herakles and Hebe, or Youth, and some statues of
the Graces which looked far older. In Argos itself there is
almost too much to see and the local guides, full of erratic
information, are a nuisance. He pays his respect to the monument of Amphiaraos, the warrior prophet who fought with
the Seven against Thebes and was taken down into Earth
which opened to receive him. Not far from the agora is a
barrow said to contain the beautiful, deadly head of the Gor-
gon Medusa which Perseus struck off and brought to Greece.
In the center of the city, quite new, the marble almost glaring
in the sunlight, Danaos sits enthroned with his fifty daughters—forty-nine, rather, for a little apart is Hypermestra, the
only one who on the fatal night following the forced marriage
to their Egyptian cousins refused to take her husband's life.
There is so much, shrines, altars, temples, emblems of divin-

ity, heroic memories. How should a man bred in such a place
not do great things? The entire city is holy ground, a sanctuary
or precinct.

Not a word of the song has yet been written down, but
all the same it is starting to take shape. There must be a long
rich section on Argos and the victor's great inheritance, probably to start with. And since Theaios has won a great many
victories and comes from a distinguished athletic family, there
must be a big victory list bristling with names and places and
prizes. Two big matching sections, then, the one arising from,
leading into, the other. Build the song out of solid blocks,
perhaps, rather than overrun and interweave.

And something else claims its place in the pattern, a cherished family tradition which the poet learns about at dinner
on his first evening in Argos. In the old days some nine or
ten generations back a maternal ancestor of the victor called
Pamphaes had the high honor of entertaining the great Twin
Horsemen Kastor and Polydeukes, the Dioskouroi, Sons of
Zeus. The room where they supped is treated as a shrine, the
scene of an annual ritual, the Hosting of the Twain. The family make it clear that they want this story worked into the
song, and rightly so—it throws a great deal of light on the
victory. Otherwise they leave the poet a pretty free hand (unlike some clients who practically try to write the song for you).
That visit was where everything began; so direct a mark of
divine favor left its impress on a family for generations and
did much to explain their athletic achievements, since the
Twins were great athletes themselves and patrons of the
games. The victory started from there; does this mean that
the song must start from there too, with a brilliant invocation
to the Sons of Zeus? Pindar had led off this way some years
back and it went very well. But how will the invocation fit in
with the mythical block which has to come first or anyway

early on? If the Twins planted the seed of victory, Argos provided the soil where it grew. No, praise of Argos must come first, a roll call of great names and the stories they call up. Argive names or at least names that with a bit of stretching can pass for Argive, whereas the Twins, though worshiped at Argos, did not come from there. Better to work them in later. As the subject of the story? Yes!

What story to tell? There's plenty of choice. Some stories are plain disreputable—the one about bride-rape, for instance—while others are too low altogether. Nothing wrong with homely incidents; they serve to set off the grand things and avoid the danger of being *too* high and mighty, but some of the tales go too far. It is said, for example, that together with another pair of brothers called Idas and Lynkeus the Twins drove off some cattle, and when the time came to divide the spoil Idas cut a cow in four parts and said that the man who ate his share first should have half of everything, the rest to go to whoever finished next. Idas then devoured his own share and his brother's as well, whereupon he and Lynkeus went off with the remaining cattle. Low stuff, nothing can be made of that, but all the same it leads to something very fine, the fight between the two pairs of brothers where Kastor got his death wound and was saved only by Polydeukes' heroic decision to give up his own immortality in return for his brother's life. This will go splendidly provided the business about the cattle rustling is handled tactfully.

There are different accounts of the Twins' nature. The poet decides for once not to follow his old master—Hesiod held that both were the sons of Zeus—but to take the version which made Polydeukes the immortal son of Zeus while Kastor, begotten by Tyndareus, was mortal. The Twins thus combine mortal and immortal. The story of their birth turns the poet's thoughts to Herakles. He was begotten when Zeus vis-

ited his mother Alkmena, after which her husband Amphitryon begot his twin brother, Iphikles. Bring this in too,
another matching pair. It applies to the victor in a way. Like
this: Herakles—a mortal who was taken up to heaven and
became immortal. The Twins—originally one mortal, the
other immortal, now both half-mortal for ever. The victor—
mortal, but with the shine of immortality that's on every
victor.

Perhaps—it's coming together fast now—perhaps lead
the opening section to a climax at the end of the first triad
with a picture of Herakles in heaven with his divine bride,
Hebe. Herakles wasn't Argive, of course, but he belongs in
any victory song and his mother Alkmena was an Argive
woman. Then end the whole song with the story of the
Twins—a grand finale with the appearance of Zeus in answer
to Polydeukes' appeal, Kastor brought back to life, and the
Twins' strange destiny, one day up there on Olympos, the
next under the earth of their native Sparta. End there—no
need for the usual return to the victor. Let the story make the
statement, indirectly, that he too has a foot in heaven from
now on. Stronger, sometimes, not to come right out with it.

There's the victory list still to think about and this always
takes a lot of work: you have to keep the pressure up all the
time or it goes dead. Theaios provided the tally of his victories, two sets in fact, his own (all to be included, of course)
and those won by members of his family and fellow Argives.
These to be treated more selectively. The man's own victories
must come first (the lot, so there's no need to go back to them
at the end), a big block coming straight after the mythical
block in praise of Argos at the start. No problem about the
transition. Simply break off with "But there's more here than
I can tell!" and then start the new triad impetuously, no connecting link. Then fill the third triad with the other victories,

touching down now here now there, a few place names, some
allusive descriptions of the prizes, some bits of landscape
maybe, and close with Pamphaes entertaining the Twins.
Then give the rest of the song to their story, two whole triads.
Theaios has paid for five, so there's plenty of room. This is
going to be a *big* work, built out of massive blocks with end-
stopped triads, not a single overrun. Strong rather than complex—plotting, language, meter, and dance movements (more
thought still needed here) all clear and brilliant. The victories
need more thought. Take a walk round the town, just look.
Leave it to the daimon.

He finds his thoughts going back to Herakles, even
though he is not going to play a big role. Perhaps *this* is why
he has to come in: Theaios is proud of his success and so he
should be, but it's clear that he has not yet got the thing he
wants more than anything in the world, the olive wreath from
Olympia, *the games Herakles founded.* This means that the usual
hope for an Olympian victory to come needs to be given special weight. Put it in the form of a prayer to Zeus? Surely, but
fairly routine. Work in a prayer but go on to suggest that it
will soon be granted. Why not use Theaios' Athenian victory
for this? Not one of the sacred games but still quite grand and
the prize is one of those great decorated vases they make
there, full of olive oil. Olive, olive wreath, Olympian victory. . . . A bit obvious maybe, but right for here. Bring second triad to a crescendo with this. Probably needs a picture.

Now for the story. In one version of the fight Polydeukes
was wounded by a stone thrown at him by Lynkeus. The poet
walks to the spot where the fight is said to have taken place,
a bit out of town, and an old man minding his sheep near
what looks like an ancient grave-mound points to a stone
which he said Lynkeus had wrenched off and hurled at Poly.
Work this in, nice local color. The old fellow is good on Lyn-

keus too, Lynx-eye he calls him. "Sharpest pair of eyes in all Greece he had. Why, they say he could see through rocks and even through the earth. That was how he caught sight of the Twins hiding in the hollow of a tree, waiting for him." Vivid stuff, should certainly be used, but it must not be allowed to overshadow the ending, which has to be high and solemn. Handle it like this: since there are two full triads left for the story, set up a clear contrast between them. The first almost pure narrative, moving fast (the dancers will enjoy that—it's the slow bits they find hard) and including more detail than usual. Make it really exciting. Then for the final triad or perhaps just at the end of the previous one, slow down and be very grand as Zeus himself appears to Poly and grants his prayer and Kastor comes back to life. Start the story at the end of course, with Poly's great decision and Kastor's death, then work back and show how it happens, other way round this time, Kastor's death first, Poly's prayer and decision second. That gives you the neat ab:BA shape. Careful plotting overlaid, almost hidden, by rich language and treatment. It always works.

Fragments of a tune, a strong dactylic beat, have been running through his head for days like an elusive memory. If he can just get the first line the pattern will start to take shape. Next day he goes to look at the Danaos monument again and it is there, standing in the morning sunlight, thinking of nothing, that it comes, at one stroke:

Danaou polin aglaothronōn te pentēkonta korān,
˘ ˘ –   ˘ ˘ – ˘˘   ˘ – ˘ – – – ˘ ˘ –

    Kharites!
    ˘ ˘ –

The fluid rising movement of the first half of the line comes suddenly up against the percussive second half where the

staccato of repeated t's and k's, and the run of long syllables,
creates its own rhythmical percussion against the metrical
ground. With the words, the opening movement of the dance
takes form before his eyes.

FOR THEAIOS OF ARGOS, THE WRESTLER*

Δαναοῦ πόλιν ἀγλαοθρόνων τε πεντήκοντα κορᾶν, Χάριτες

A.1. City of Dánaos and his fifty daughters
          modeled in sunlight on your carved thrones!
      Sing this city, Graces, it is Hera's,
      home for a god's presence, flaming
      with glory for all the brave things done.
      Perseus and Medusa—that is a long story,
      or the count of cities Épaphos founded in Egypt,
      or Hyperméstra who went straight when all her sisters
          strayed.
      Hers was the only sword
                      kept to its scabbard and voted no.

  2. And Diomédes, the great gray-eyed Athena
          made him a deathless god.
      And Amphiaráos, prophet, battle's stormcloud—
      God's bolt struck the Theban earth
          open to take him.
      And the women, so many beautiful women
      in the old days. Zeus came to Dánaë's bed
                          and to Alkména.

  3. He nerved Amphítryon's spear. A fortunate man,
      won kinship with Zeus. For when that bronze-age
          hero

*The translation is somewhat freer than elsewhere and some names of
persons and places have been omitted.

left for war, the Lord assumed his likeness
and came with fathering seed—Herakles!
whose bride is Youth. She walks by Hera's side
    in heaven, a lovely goddess.

B.1. Too much for my tongue's telling
all the fine things this Argive precinct holds
and men are quick to cry That's praise enough!
Yet rouse the lyre to song
    and set in your mind the image of a wrestler.
You have seen on Hera's day
    the people crowd to the Game for the Bronze
    Shield
                ritual slaughter of oxen
                athletes brought to the test.
It was there that Oúlias' son
                  Theaios
won twice, and, winning, earned
forgetfulness of all that he'd endured.

  2. This man outdid the best that Greece could send to
    Delphi
        and took the Pythian crown.
Off to the Isthmos next, his luck still on him.
    Three times victor there by the Gates of the Sea
    Three times victor on Neméa's holy ground
he gave the Muses a broad field to plough.
Zeus, father! his heart's deep longing
    finds no issue in speech.
But the end of all action is yours.
With a spirit that shirks no labor
and daring to match,
          he asks your favor, Lord.

3. Do I sing things hidden from God and the man who
       strains
   for the athlete's utmost reach? Far beyond all is
   Herakles' founding, Olympia. Yet sweetly
   preludial voices hailed his triumph at Athens
   twice. And their fired earth brought the olive's fruit
   to this brave land of Hera
              in the great jar's patterned hold.

C.1. Honor attends your mother's clan, Theaios,
     so clear the report of their conquests,
              the Graces aiding and the Sons of Zeus.
     Were that stock mine
              I'd not walk Argos' streets with downcast eyes.
     Again, again, victory has broken into flower!
     Four times in the gulf of Corinth
              and the games at Neméa.

2. And which was the field your Argive prizemen left,
          their cups'
                      silver upon them
   or shouldering the fleece-lined coats they'd won?
   Enumerate every glitter of their bronze spoils?
          The tally would strain time's bounds,
   all Kleitor awarded, all that Tegéa gave
          and the hill towns of Akhaia
   or Mount Lykáon where by God's track stood the
       prize
   for strong hand's seizure or the outpacing foot.

3. Since the Sons of Zeus
              Kastor and his brother Polydeúkes
   were hosted by your forbear Pámphaës,
   small wonder this house has bred a race of athletes.

Marshals of the dancing lawns of Sparta,
with Hermes and Lord Herakles they tend
the ceremony of the games and keep them green.
They care for all good men.
> The gods do not break faith.

D.1. Turn and turn about, those two
pass one day with their loving father Zeus,
deep in the hollows of Sparta's earth the next,
a single lot for both. This life,
sooner than all a god and live in heaven,
Polydeúkes chose when Kastor fell.
It was Idas' spear that brought him down. Idas
was angry. There was some quarrel about cattle.

2. His brother Lynx-Eye
(sharpest eyes in all Greece)
marked the two heroes sitting in the trunk of an oak
tree.
So Lynx-Eye and brother Idas hurried over
ready for a famous fight. And dreadfully
they suffered at the hands of Zeus. In a flash
Poly was on them. They turned and fought
beside their father's tomb and one

3. seizing an enwrought death-stone flung it straight
at Polydeúkes. It did not crush him
or force him back. He charged, and drove
his bronze-tipped javelin straight through Lynx-Eye's
chest
and Zeus's smoking thunderbolt fell clean on Idas.
They burned in that lonely place
together.
> Hard fighting with your betters.

E.1. Then quickly Polydeúkes
went back to where his brother Kastor lay
not dead yet but the last
ruckling breath shuddered his whole frame.
In tears he called to Zeus: "Father,
no end to pain? Please, let me die too
here with my brother. Honor leaves a man
whose friend has gone and there are few to trust

2. when trouble comes." And Zeus
was with him, face to face. "You are my son.
It was mortal seed that fell for this man's birth
after I left your mother.
Listen, I give you this choice. You may escape death
and hard old age to live with me in heaven,
with Ares that dark spearman and Athena.

3. This can be yours. But if you choose your brother's
part,
go even with him in everything,
you must live half beneath the earth,
half in the golden places of the sky."
He spoke. And Polydeúkes saw his way at once.
He opened Kastor's eyes and gave him back his voice,
bronze-armored Kastor.

IV THE HARMONIES
OF LOVE AND RULE

Pythian 9: Qui Regna Amore

A POEM MARKED EVERYWHERE BY SPEED, PYTHIAN 9 GETS
down to business at once:

> I long to proclaim him!
>   He took the Pythian crown, a bronzeshield runner—
> and the Graces join in my cry
>   that garlands Kyrána:
> this fortunate man Telesíkrates.

Then, the familiar turn on the relative pronoun at its most
breathtaking, Kyrana the city (which) becomes Kyrana the
wild huntress, *parthenos agrotera* (*la belle sauvage*, Norwood),
who in the wind-crackling gorges of her native Thessaly was
taken in love by Apollo and brought to the place where her
future city would rise. Aphrodite was there to receive them,
an appropriate personage to welcome the lovers, the more so
since she had a precinct or garden in Kyrana, and "fastened
jointly for god and girl the marriage that made them one,"
but the Greek words are too amorously entwined to permit
the disjuncture of translation. Pindar now moves back more
steeply in time to the primal days when Olympos was no more
than a bare rock as he tells of the girl's ancestry. Her father
was Hupseus, High One,

King of the insolent Lapiths,
a hero second in descent
from Ocean. The naiad Mighty
who had pleasured with the river god Peneíos
in the folds of Pindos bore him,

Earth's daughter.

The narrative next swings forward to Kyrana and her hunting exploits. Disdaining normal feminine pursuits, like plying the loom or suppers with stay-at-home girlfriends, she passed her nights killing wild beasts, "granting a deep peace to her father's herds, but that sweet bedfellow that comes over the eyelids at dawn—on sleep she spent but a little time." The words are disposed in such a way that the erotic theme which is to play so large a part in this poem is suggested even as it is denied. Then, having begun the story at a point just before its conclusion and told us something about Kyrana, the poet circles back to the beginning, and the second triad opens with Apollo watching her fight a lion unarmed and single-handed.

Apart from the victory list, which is long and brilliantly intricate, Pythian 9 is an easy poem. The language presents few difficulties, and the mythical element occupying two thirds of the work—there are two myths, Kyrana's and a brief one at the end—is colored as richly and sensuously as a Titian *poesia* and is instantly appealing. And yet critics have raised the question of the poem's unity. Farnell found that it "altogether lacks unity" but apparently thought that this added to its attraction; Hermann Fränkel believed that the reader, at least on a first approach, is "troubled by the absence of any unity," and thought it best to turn to other odes before "grappling with this question" (*Early Greek Poetry and Philosophy*, 450). I wonder. I don't want to advocate Douglas Bush's curious tactic with Milton's syntax (it never worries those who leave it alone), but perhaps if we had not made such an issue of the unity of the Pindaric ode it would never have bulked so large. Move gently around and within this poem, listening to the way it breathes, watching for recurrent images or motifs, and part will begin answering to part and the design reveal itself readily enough. The problem with Pythian 9, if one exists, is very different. Abounding, ebullient, as perhaps no other work of Pindar's, the poem takes a great deal of living up to. Much of the time one is simply too dull for it.

The best course is to attend to the immediate impression it makes, to what is uppermost. A poem's surface is often conterminous with its deeps. As everyone has noticed, the love interest is central, and older critics liked to speculate on the victor's matrimonial intentions (a prothalamion as well as an epinician, Gildersleeve suggested). But since there is no evidence whatever for such speculation, it may be more profitable to have in mind something I discussed in the first chapter, Pindar's way of speaking of victory in the language of love and the conceit of victory as bride. Glancingly present in ode after ode, this sexual imagery is here explicit and pervasive. Apollo brought Kyrana as his bride to Libya (a person, again, not a place) who "will receive her gladly," *dexetai . . . prophrōn*; Telesikrates brings from Delphi the *doxan himertan* of his victory, "the glory men yearn for," to Kyrana, now queen of her city, who "will receive him kindly," *euphrōn dexetai*. The second myth is still more explicit, for here the subject is actually a bride-race. The bride-to-be is stationed in all her finery at the finishing post, the prize of whoever "thrusting forward [*thorōn*, a verb that can be used of the male mounting and impregnating the female] touches her dress." Such imagery, I suggested, is one of Pindar's ways of expressing something that otherwise would be scarcely expressible, the astounding joy which victory grants and, beyond that, the

more abundant life it brings to the whole community. The city
bursts into blossom with the achievements of her sons, Pindar
likes to say; the song which celebrates those achievements
waters the roots of the city or family tree and makes the life-
giving ancestral origins actual again. It may then be misleading to speak of the conceit of victory as bride; later critical
terms do not fit Pindar's poetry very well, which is more
literal than we can imagine.

Whatever term should be used, bridal victory, embodied
in the splendid person of Kyrana, plays a dominant role in
the poem. To date, the archaeological record reveals little or
no cult of such a figure at this time, and it may be that Pindar
has done what he does elsewhere with overseas clients whose
region lacked the religious or heroic presences his imagination
required. Borrowing from Hesiod the story of a Thessalian
huntress called Kyrana, he may have used the chance simi-
larity of the name to provide the Libyan city with a grand
ancestral heroine from the Greek mainland (See François
Chamoux, *Cyrène sous la monarchie des Battiades* [Paris, 1953],
127, 276–79). This at all events is how he treats her and this,
for the poem, is what matters. Her figure is central there and
her marriage with the great god is the principal action. By
noting how the poem shapes this action we may come to
understand its larger intentions and see how what Fränkel
calls its "motley material and disparate connexions" compose
a unified whole.

Watching Kyrana wrestle with a lion, Apollo calls to Kheiron, the wise and benignant centaur who resides in those
parts, and bids him admire the girl's courage. Who was her
father, he asks:

> torn from what stock
> does she hold the hollows of the shadowing hills?

The verb "torn" seems oddly violent and the scholiast steps in to explain that it is metaphorical: Kyrana is a branch torn from a tree. No doubt he is right, in part at least, since the Greek word for "stock," *phutla*, is cognate with *phuton*, plant or tree, and yet here too Pindar's thinking may be disconcertingly literal. Kyrana is part of the natural world, detached (torn) from it by her active human will, but still very close to it. Like others of her kind, she will originally have been a nature goddess, mother of wild beasts and all life, as we see more clearly after her marriage. You will take her to Libya as your bride, Kheiron tells Apollo, and make her queen of a city. There, transplanted to a new fertile land ("all the fruits of the seasons are hers and kinship with beasts"), Kyrana is fully reunited with the natural world from which in her virginal days she was partly reft. The child she is to bear will be entrusted to the Seasons and to Earth who will feed him with ambrosia and nectar and make him immortal. He will be called Hunter and Shepherd, "an ever-present guardian of flocks."

Kyrana can assume this role only after her union with Apollo and it is at this point that we find we are getting seriously out of our depth, for the meaning, the religious meaning, of the *hieros gamos* or sacred marriage is scarcely accessible now except as a piece of book learning. Our difficulty is increased by the evident gaiety of the scene. "Is it lawful," Apollo asks Kheiron, "to lay a famous hand upon her and reap the honey-sweet grass of her bed?" The metaphor, serving further to identify Kyrana with the natural world, is unusual and this makes the tone even harder to catch. Is this, one wonders, groping, remotely like a youthful Louis XIV humorously enquiring of a courtier whether it would be in order to seduce a milkmaid? Hardly, for the word I translated "lawful" (*hosia*) belongs to religion and what

Apollo is asking may be something like "Am I sanctioned by divine law to make this girl my own?" An odd question, odder still when we reflect that for earlier Greek thinking the answer was overwhelmingly yes. For this charming young lover who is about to take Kyrana to himself is one of the lords of life, and it is in the course of this scene that Kheiron, playfully reproaching Apollo for his pretended ignorance of the girl's birth, speaks the splendid verses in praise of his powers:

> You ask of the girl's race, Lord? You who know
> the appointed end of all things and all their ways;
> the count of leaves earth bears in spring, the sands
> of the sea and the rivers, driven by wave and wind,
> what is to be and the source of its being.
> All this is in your ken.

To accept that a great religious mystery, the marriage of heaven and earth, does not call for a subfusc Sunday morning demeanour may not, now that sex has been liberated, seem to require too great an effort of dis- and re-orientation. The day has passed when a Farnell, for whom religion could only mean his own brand of Christian monotheism, was able to describe the sacred marriage as one of the "strange illusions of the unchecked anthropomorphic imagination." And yet the loves of Apollo and Kyrana, remote as they are from the sexual restrictions we have recently stepped out of, may be no less remote from the empty permissiveness we have stepped into.

All this may seem to be making heavy weather of a brilliant scene, yet some labor of *dépaysement* is called for if we are to come to our older literature as anything more than philologists or technicians. It is only by entering, so far as we are able, into the spirit of the poem's principal action, the divine marriage, that we can understand the relation of myth to victory and the design of the whole composition. Consider the sequence of events in this central third triad. The birth of the divine child is foretold and then, the pace quickening as the myth moves to its conclusion, we have the solemn, joyful moment when the lovers "lay together in a golden chamber in Libya, and there"—abruptly we pass into the sphere of athletics—"she rules over a beautiful city famous for contests." Then comes a second praise of Telesikrates' Pythian victory, followed by the formidable parade of his previous successes. The transition from religion to sport may seem strange to us, but for Pindar it has its inexorable logic: it is *because* of the sacred marriage and the powers then bred into the race that an athlete from Kyrana can triumph so splendidly. Another way of putting it is to say that Kyrana's full *floraison* comes with her marriage, marriage that is the emblem of victory, victory which makes the city flower with the great acts of her sons. Taking seriously what Pindar took seriously is not just an interesting exercise in comparative religion; it is the only way of making sense of his poetry.

And now it is time for the part of the ode which Telesikrates and his family must have been waiting for. The poet would have been given a list of the victories to praise; his task was to dispose them in such a way that each one stood out with its special luster. Epinician connoisseurs too would have been keenly interested in what was coming. Any competent singer could belt you out a good stretch of narrative or some routine praise, but a big victory list was something else and needed a master's touch. There must be periphrasis, of course, the bare enumeration of places and prizes heightened into something rich and strange; there has to be constant variation with a moment from myth or an exquisite landscape detail, a prayer perhaps, an apt sententia or two, the whole thing handled with an air of magnanimous ease that does not conceal and isn't meant to conceal the difficulty of what is being done. The modern reader, it is to be feared, finds himself less stimulated and is likely to look on the victory list as something he must put up with for the sake of those parts of an ode that still work for him. It is all very well for David Young to protest stoutly, "I am not bored by the catalogue of victories but awed." What is required is not simply to accept the Greek cult of physical excellence but to recover a poetic taste that was on its way out in the early eighteenth century. If you have to say "cut the crust off the loaf," Pope and Swift tell the bad poet in their *Peri Bathous,* you must write "strip white Ceres of her nut-brown Coat." And yet this seemingly trite device has been a source of real poetic pleasure. Has been, and still can be in the hands of a poet. In Pope's hands: "And China's Earth receives the smoking Tyde." (Tea is poured.) And in Pindar's: "Thebes of the Seven Gates saw that Iolaos too honored him." The bare statement (Telesikrates also won in the Theban games called the Iolaia) is first elevated by periphrasis, then enlivened with a few lines of heroic ornamentation: "Iolaos, after he had shorn off the head of Eurystheus with the sword's edge, they buried in the tomb where his forefather lay, the charioteer Amphitryon who came to dwell with the Sown Men in the streets of Kadmos where they ride white horses." Although a few notes can fill in the background painlessly enough, our unfamiliarity with the poet's material does unfortunately impede the pleasure he wants to give us. Pleasure, and something else, for to an imagination like Pindar's this heroic past is present. Legend told how Iolaos returned to life to punish Eurystheus for his injurious treatment of Herakles; he is pictured as coming to life again to watch Telesikrates' performance in his games, which is a new act of heroic *virtù*.

The mention of Amphitryon leads to his wife Alkmena who bore twin sons, as we heard in Nemean 10, Herakles and Iolaos' father Iphikles, the first to Zeus, the second to her husband. The poet praises Herakles, always his paragon of excellence, and with a prayer to the Graces ("May the clear light of the clamorous Graces not fail me!") passes to further victories his client won at Aigina and Megara: "At Aigina, I declare, and by the hill of Nisos three times you glorified this city." Since the city must be Kyrana (Wilamowitz confused the issue for nearly half a century by insisting that it was Thebes), it is best to take the lines that follow as describing Telesikrates' triumphs in the games of his native country. More important than the location, however, is the passage itself, a little scene in which the heroic tone that is proper to a victory list gives way to a note of tender, sensual longing as we are shown not the victor scoring one more success but women watching him succeed—just as in the myth, with a reversal of the sexes, Apollo gazed with amorous wonder as Kyrana wrestled with the lion. Let the lines stand first in their original Greek since there is such a madrigal sweetness in the syntax that translation is an impertinence:

πλεῖστα νικάσαντά σε καὶ τελεταῖς
ὡρίαις ἐν Παλλάδος εἶδον ἄφωνοί
   θ' ὡς ἕκασται φίλτατον
παρθενικαὶ πόσιν ἢ
υἱὸν εὔχοντ', ὦ Τελεσίκρατες, ἔμμεν.

And often, as you won at the seasonal
Rites of Pallas they watched you and, speechless

each in her fashion O
     dearest   husband
           girls their
           or mothers
their son, Telesíkrates, prayed that you might be.

(The meaning may be rather that girls prayed to win such a husband or bear such a son. I follow the scholiast's interpretation.)

The parade of Telesikrates' victories fills the whole of the fourth triad and spills over into the beginning of the fifth. One expects the poem to end soon after this, with some reminder of mortal limitation, perhaps, or an image of vicissitude. Instead, for nothing in this exultant work is allowed to check the thrust of joy, "someone" reminds the poet as he "quenches his thirst for song," still unslaked, of a debt as yet unpaid and bids him awaken an ancient glory of the race. At this, with a new surge of energy, Pindar launches into another complete though briefer myth. Drawn from local folklore, the tale is of how one Antaios staged for his daughter a bride-race in which all the notables of the region competed for her hand. It is as if it were a replay of the main myth, a more explicit treatment of the theme of victory as bride, and is related to the main myth by some clear verbal links. Pindar ennobles this obscure African story by neatly boxing it inside the story of another bride-race in mainland Greece, one staged by Danaos of Argos for his forty-eight daughters. The winner here will be an ancestor of Telesikrates, and the myth—and the poem—ends picturesquely as "hand in hand he led the stately girl through the ranks of nomad horsemen."

Many were the leaves they flung
and many the garlands.
Many the victory wings he had won before.

Exquisitely, the poem melts into its occasion for, as it ends, the chorus (we may suppose) joins the audience and together they throw leaves over the victor in salutation of his triumph. Floating above and about him the leaves are like the wings of birds—the wings that, in the lines of Theognis which Pindar seems to have known well, carry a man's fame over land and sea and grant him immortality. The passage strangely resembles Petrarch's loveliest vision of Laura sitting in a cloud of flowers that circle around her and mark her as a blessed presence, goddess of the realm of love: *Qui regna Amore.** An appropriate legend for this poem composed in a fortunate hour under the sign of Aphrodite and performed, one would like to think, in her Cyrenean garden, as Pythian 5 seems to have been.

Pythian 1: A Rich and Lordly Crown

From Pindar at his happiest to Pindar at his grandest. Composed in 470, four years before the poem we have just read, Pythian 1, for Hieron lord of Syracuse, is with Olympian 1 the most famous and admired of the poet's surviving works. Here if anywhere is the sublime Pindar of tradition, sailing with supreme dominion through the azure deep of air, from another perspective the "big rhetorical drum" to which Pound objected. Not that the language is inflated: it is too energetic for that. Writing for the richest and most powerful man in the

---

*Da' be' rami scendea,
  dolce ne la memoria,
  una pioggia di fior sovra 'l suo grembo . . .
  qual fior cadea sul lembo,
  qual su le treccie bionde . . .
  qual si posava in terra e qual su l'onde,
  qual con un vago errore
  girando parea dir: "Qui regna Amore."

Greek world, Pindar very deliberately set out to give him what he obviously wanted, a big poem. "Magni nunc erat oris opus." A big poem, and an exceptionally unified one; the clarity of the design no doubt explains some of its popularity. "Never were the parts of a great and complex ode more organically welded together," wrote Farnell, usually so baffled by Pindar's poetic structures. Though there is much in Pythian 1 that remains archaic, it is approaching the classical sense of form and has thus satisfied those for whom form could only be classical form. This is a great poem, certainly, and yet anyone who has acquired a feeling for the older, preclassical kind of design and who cherishes Pindar the master of the delicate style will always find something lacking here and turn with relief to the poems he wrote for the ancient communities of mainland Greece and Aigina, characterized by what John H. Finley calls their "tone of ease and at-homeness" (*Pindar and Aeschylus* [1966], 30).

Pythian 1 opens with an invocation to the lyre: "Golden Lyre, rightful possession of Apollo and the Muses! The foot that steps off into splendor hears you and the singers wait for the cue from your trembling strings as you strike up the prelude to the dance." But for the opening word, we would take this as an unusually vivid description of the performance that is just beginning, something that Pindar quite often gives us. The fact that the lyre is golden, however, shows that this is no earthly celebration, for gold is the attribute of the gods, the substance of which everything they handle is made. The scene is Olympos and we may recall the beautiful passage in the Homeric hymn to Apollo where the god, "stepping high and fine," plays the lyre as the Muses raise their antiphonal song and the Graces and Hours dance with the other daughters of heaven. However, this hymn to the lyre, whose music pervades the universe, has an intellectual even metaphysical range far beyond the brilliant immediacy of the Homeric hymn. We hear first how its music acts upon the turbulent powers associated with Zeus, then of its effect on "those whom Zeus does not love." It soothes the breast of violent Ares and lulls to sleep Zeus's mighty messenger, the eagle. This can be taken fairly literally, but when the lyre is said to "quench the everlasting flame of warrior thunderbolt," it is clear that its music must be understood figuratively or symbolically. The lyre is in fact a *symbol* for something, not a word normally required for Pindar. This becomes still clearer in the lines devoted to the adversary powers, chief among them the hundred-headed monster Typhon, "the enemy of the gods," who in Hesiod's account challenged Zeus after he, with the other gods, had overcome the Titans. "A thing past help would have happened" and Typhon become master of heaven and earth had not Zeus defeated him in single combat and then assumed supreme dominion, allotting to the other gods their several provinces and offices (*Theogony*, 820–885). Pindar does not describe this conflict, not so much because Hesiod had done it for him but because here it is Zeus's "music," the music of the lyre, rather than the terror of his red right hand, which subdues Typhon. What Pindar does is to show the extent of Zeus's victory and the danger threatening the sum of things by describing the being he vanquished. Typhon lies beneath Mount Aitna, his huge snakish body extending as far as Kuma, just above Naples, defeated but still potent. A few years before the performance of the ode Aitna had erupted, and Pindar opens the second triad with a portentous description of the volcano in action that is at the same time a mythological picture of the fire-breathing monster beneath it:

> Sky high the pillared steep of Aitna's cruel snow,
> her yearlong charge, weighs on him,

> while from her deeps she belches
>   dread springs of holy fire.
> By day, rivers of flameshot smoke
> course down her slopes while in night's dark
> the red tide sends boulders clattering
>   to the sea's face far below.
> So fearfully the fire-worm spouts! a wonder
> to watch him, wonderful even to hear of,
> pinioned under Aitna's black and leafy peaks
> bedded on the spikes that goad his back.

"Those whom Zeus does not love," Pindar says, "flee in terror when they hear the voice of the Muses." The music which quells destructive, chaotic forces of this kind must be something like cosmic harmony, a principle of order and proportion which keeps the elements in tune. To put it in Platonic terms, it is thanks to this music that we speak of a *kosmos*, world order, rather than an *akosmia* or world disorder (*Gorgias* 508a). The fact that one is drawn to invoke Plato at this point suggests that Pindar is moving out of his customary sphere and that something very grand or grandiose is being proposed.

And the poem is unusual in other respects. We are almost a third of the way in, and so far there has been no mention of victor or victory, nothing to show that this is an epinician. It is, composed to celebrate a chariot victory by Hieron, and Pindar does not neglect the epinician occasion. Yet it is clear that Hieron's achievements in other fields claim an equal perhaps greater attention and, to be understood, require the massive prelude. With great skill Pindar now proceeds to bind together his different themes. The picture of Typhon is at once followed by a prayer to Zeus: Zeus who rules over Mount Aitna beneath which the monster lies, Zeus who alone can keep him in subjection; Aitna at whose foot lies a new city,

also called Aitna, which has just been founded by Hieron;
Hieron whose victory in the Pythian conquest augurs well for
the new foundation:

> May we find favor in your eyes, O Zeus. You rule
> this mount of Aitna, forefront of a fruitful land,
> Aitna whose namesake city
> the famous founder glorified
> the day the herald at the Pythian games
> pronounced this city's name and Hieron's name,
>
> chariot victor!

With this, we find ourselves in more familiar epinician territory, with a prayer for further victories and an invocation to
Apollo, god of the Pythian games.

But not for long. After some conventional lines in praise
of Hieron, a new theme is introduced, his bravery in war:

> Time surely will bring back to him
> how steadfast in the battle line he stood
> when he and his plucked by God's grant
> > honor as no Greek else,
> a rich and lordly crown.

And a rich and lordly Greek phrase, *ploutou stephanōm' age-
rōkhon*, that might stand as the emblem of this poem. Pindar
now interweaves these two themes, Hieron as city-founder
and as soldier, combining them with his official epinician
theme and introducing another figure, Hieron's son Deinomenes, king of the new city. This must have been one of the
poet's most complex commissions and the plotting is unusually tight. He bids the Muse

> stand too by Deinómenes' side
> as you chant the reward for Hieron's team of horses.

The father's joy is the son's.
Come now, we must fashion in friendship a song for
    Aitna's king.

For him Hieron laid out this city,
    god-founded in freedom,
on the old Dorian plan.

We hear briefly of the deeds of the founders of the Dorian
tribes in the days when "the fame of their spears burst into
blossom." In typically archaic fashion Pindar conceives that
the way to create something new is to return to the origins.
There follows one more prayer to Zeus for the new foundation
and the hope that Hieron will lead the people into "the harmony of peace." On this significant phrase Pindar turns again
to war, very much in the manner of Milton's "But drive farr
off the barbarous dissonance. . . ."

Grant I beseech you, Lord, that quietly
the Carthaginian and the Etruscan keep
their battle-yammer home now they have seen
the shiploss keening warlust brought them to off Kuma,
the blows they suffered at our captain's hand
when from the scudding decks he flung their youth
to drown seadeep, wrenching
        the slavish yoke from our Greek necks.

The sea battle of Kuma in which Hieron defeated the Etrus-
cans took place in 474. The triad ends with a battle fought six
years earlier at Himera in northern Sicily where Hieron and
his brothers defeated the Carthaginians. Between his allu-
sions to these two victories, whereby Sicilian princes de-
fended the southwestern frontiers of Hellas against the
barbaroi, Pindar sets the two more celebrated battles of Salamis
and Plataia in which mainland Greeks rolled back the might

of Persia. There is in these lines a pan-Hellenic vision, a sense of the unity not simply cultural but political of the Greek world, which is often denied to Pindar and which indeed he nowhere else shows so clearly.

The function of the prelude and the design of the poem as a whole are coming clear. Hieron's victories at Kuma and Himera recall Zeus's victory over Typhon in the primal days: Typhon whose vast frame stretches from Sicily to Kuma. And when we hear of Hieron's work in establishing the harmony of peace, we think of the greater harmony established in the universe by Zeus, symbolically represented in the hymn to the lyre. An analogy is being set up between Zeus's cosmogonic victory over the chaos demon and Hieron's earthly victories over the barbarians (as Greeks saw them). And there is surely another no less far-reaching analogy: between Hieron's foundation of a new city and Zeus's refounding of the shattered universe after the battle with Typhon. This is not described in the ode: it does not need to be. The great mythological paradigms are built so solidly into human consciousness that any one part can be counted on to call up the others. When we are told that the chaos demon has been defeated, we know that the consolidation of the cosmos is at hand. Equally, any human founding can always be seen as an analogue of the divine foundational act. When the poet of *Beowulf* tells of the building of the great hall Hierot and of the celebration marking the occasion, the song which the minstrel then sings can have only one theme. He must tell

> . . . how the Almighty made the earth-fields
> Brilliant in beauty, bound by the sea,
> Set exulting sun and moon
> As lamps for the light of living men.
> (*Beowulf* [trans. Edwin Morgan, 1962], 92–95)

No less paradigmatically required, the building of Hierot and the creation hymn celebrated there at once provoke the anger of the outcast spirit Grendel, "God's adversary," as he wanders the dark moors and drive him to attack the new human settlement. Similarly in Pindar's ode, celebration in heaven—the sound of the lyre, the Muses' singing—is at once followed by or rather leads to, must lead to, the monster's furious outburst in the nether regions.

Victorious general in war, farsighted ruler in peace, Hieron's accomplishments can hardly go further, and at this point Pindar breaks off with some appropriate epinician sentiments (Speak in season, Keep your discourse tight with much in little, Avoid the praise that stirs up envy), and devotes the final triad to what amounts to a portrait of the ideal prince. This takes the form of a series of precepts addressed, it seems likely, to Deinomenes and set peremptorily side by side: "Steer the tribe with the tiller of Justice. Forge your tongue on truth's anvil. Your lightest word goes forth in power; many mark you, for good or ill. Like a wise pilot, let out your sail to the breeze," and so forth. Pindar is not lecturing the young man or preaching to him; he is praising him and at one remove praising his august father. These precepts do not so much tell him what he should do as describe what he, as a just prince, does do. After the excitement and magnificence of all that has gone before, the conclusion cannot but seem (at least to a modern reader) something of an anticlimax, but it is finely done and eminently Pindaric. Characteristically skillful is the way the final precept, "Do not be deceived by shifty gain" (that is, do not count the cost—engage the services of a front-rank poet), leads to the thought of the fame that lives on and reveals to chroniclers and poets the pattern of a life. This is at once translated in the archaic fashion into contrasting pictures of the good and bad king. On the one hand Kroisos, whose kindly virtue does not fade, on the other the tyrant Phalaris, who roasted his subjects in a bronze bull and won not fame but infamy, "nor do lyres in hall admit him to gentle concert with the singing of boys." Beautifully echoing the opening hymn to the lyre, the words have the delicacy, in Pindar's own language ἀβρότας, of Milton's "airs and madrigals that whisper softnes in chambers," striking a welcome note in this poem so full of pride and splendor. One rather wishes it could have ended here, but some final lines in praise of Hieron were needed and for this Pindar returns to the grand manner: "Good fortune is the first of prizes, a good name the second. But he who wins and keeps them both: his is the highest crown."

Unusual in several respects, Pythian 1 is unusual in this too, that the myth does not stand in the normal relation to the official subject, Hieron's chariot victory—welcome evidence that, strict as the rules of the epinician convention may have been, the poet was not their servant but their master and could bend them to the needs of the occasion. The pattern of this poem, if we stand back from it, is clear and powerful. Hieron's athletic victory, though not neglected, is clearly subordinate to his military and civil achievements. The divine paradigm to which these achievements are related—the music of the heavenly lyre and Zeus's overthrow of Typhon—represents (again, one is tempted to say symbolizes) the disruptive forces which a successful ruler must overcome and the steps he must take to establish the ordered harmony of peace. To propose an analogy not simply between earthly and cosmic order but between Hieron and Zeus is bold but, given the grandiose scope of this poem, the analogy may reach even farther than we have yet seen. What if the Olympian festivities in the prelude are celebrating Zeus's victory over Typhon and are thus the archetype of all victory celebration? A line that has drifted down to us among the flotsam of the post-Homeric epic tradition suggests that the poetic record knew of such an occasion, when Zeus himself danced:

In their midst the father of gods and men danced.

This line, it has been conjectured, occurred in a poem describing the joyful ceremony that took place on Olympos after the defeat of the Titans (See G. L. Huxley, *Greek Epic Poetry from Eumelos to Panyassis* [1969], 124). It would be a small step to advance these solemnities a little and suppose that they marked the occasion when Zeus defeated the most formidable foe of all, Typhon. Directly to compare the present celebration for Hieron with the festal day in heaven when the gods hailed the final establishment of the cosmos would have been too much even for Pindar, but in poetry indirection is often more effective and simply to hint at this supreme relation would be praise of the highest order. One may play with the fancy that, the performance ended, Hieron, catching his audacious poet's point, stood up and joining the dancers executed a few steps himself. But that might have brought divine resentment down on his head and anyway it appears that he was not a perceptive literary critic. He is said to have preferred Bacchylides to Pindar.

V QUESTIONS OF INTERPRETATION

Nemean 4: Feigned Foes and Singers Outre-Tombe

I BEGAN THE FIRST CHAPTER BY CLAIMING THAT PINDAR IS less difficult than his reputation would indicate. The main difficulty is that the genre we chiefly know him by, the victory ode, is so unlike anything found in later literature. Some odes do of course raise real problems of interpretation, but for the purpose of this book, which is to suggest that Pindar is a fine enough poet to deserve the attention of anyone who cares for poetry, there was no need to tackle them; they belong to more specialized studies. I needed only to assemble a reasonably representative set of interesting poems and try to show how they work. The poems to be discussed in this chapter do, however, present certain problems in whole or in part, intrinsic or extrinsic. By an extrinsic problem I mean one that has come about through the recent shift in Pindaric criticism which denies the presence in a text of something formerly taken to be there in light of which it was understood.

There is nothing difficult about the opening of Nemean 4. It begins quietly, thoughtfully, with a statement taking the form of a homely conceit: Joy, the joy of victory celebration, is the "best healer of toil surmounted." Doctor Joy is assisted by nurses, "songs, the wise daughters of the Muses, who charm away toil by their touch." Still more homely: "Not even hot water soothes the limbs like praise joined to the lyre."

111

Conceit then gives way to bare memorable utterance: "The word lives longer than the act, whatever by gift of the Graces tongue draws up from deep mind." The victory poem is more than hurt labor's bath, more than a reward for the ardors of training or a balm for strained muscles and bruised limbs. It heals a greater hurt, the hurt of mortality. For the trouble with victory, as with all great achievement, is that it does not last; a brief flash and it is over or, as Herodotos says, it goes out. The word, though it must remain unspoken until called forth by the act, can give the act a measure of permanence. The games began as funeral celebrations for Heroes and even if by Pindar's day they had taken on a different, larger role, he never forgot that the ultimate purpose and power of the victory ode was to protect the victor from his mortality, insofar as that was possible. At the end of one ode, recalling how he saw the triumphant young athlete standing by an altar at Olympia, he says with what to our distant ears sounds like sudden passion: "He was beautiful and touched by that grace of youth which once kept shameless death from Ganymede" (Olympian 10).

The first stanza is over and so far we have learned only that a victory has taken place. We do not know who won it or where, in what contest, or where the victory came from. Nor do we know how far into the body of the ode the statement made by the prelude is going to extend, hence how much weight to give it. There has been only one regular epinician element, one that meant a great deal to Pindar: an affirmation of poetry's power to praise. Our first set of questions the new stanza answers at once, and perhaps it says something to our second. This is a Nemean victory, the athlete's name is Timasarkhos, he won the wrestling match, and a handsome periphrasis reveals where he came from: "May the walled home of the Aiakidai receive my song, beacon for all of guest and stranger right." He came from Aigina. The victor's father is named next, but not simply named: "If your father Timokritos were still warmed by the raging Sun," Pindar says, "often, bowed over the song as his fingers drew now this note now that from the strings, he would have celebrated his victorious son. . . ." The dead father, then, was a musician and perhaps something of a poet too (later we hear that the whole clan was devoted to epinician poetry), for we find that the next stanza, which provides the first victory list, carries on without a break so that it could be part of what the father would have sung: ". . . his victorious son who from the contest at Nemea brought home a chain of garlands and from famous Athens and. . . ." In other odes we learn that the dead have some share in the joy of victory celebration; here, since there is no way of knowing how far the father's song extends, it seems that the dead can compose victory poetry themselves. Another conceit, we suppose, and an unusual one, expressed by a device itself somewhat unusual, a song within a song, although Pindar does use the same device, more clearly, in Nemean 5 where the singer is Apollo in person.

The first two victories, at Nemea and Athens, are given fairly straight. For the third, a picture: ". . . and at Thebes of the Seven Gates, by Amphiaraos' shining tomb the sons of Kadmos gladly wreathed him in flowers, for Aigina's sake." Aigina and Thebes, bound by cultural and political ties and also by mythological kinship (their ancestral heroines were sisters), are bound now by the fact that a Theban poet is praising an Aiginetan victor: "A friend among friends, he gazed at the welcoming city as he went toward the famous house of Herakles. . . ." The mention of Herakles leads, by the linking relative which Pindar loves to use for this purpose, to the myth: Herakles, "with whom strong Telamon

once. . . ." Telamon, one of the sons of Aiakos, went with the
great Theban hero on an earlier campaign against Troy, took
the city and at some cost overcame the giant Alkyoneus. In
the usual account the protagonist was Herakles and that is
the version Pindar relates in Isthmian 6. But myth was malle-
able, a narrative matrix rather than a fixed corpus, and a poet
could within limits fashion it as he chose. Here, Pindar emphasizes the role played not by Herakles but by the Aiginetan
hero Telamon. The story is told briefly but with plenty of
punch, then Pindar adds: "He who has had a taste of battle
will catch my drift. Who does must take his knocks." Why
the comment? To show the bearing of this ancestral geste on
today's victor: he too has taken his knocks and song is now
charming them away with its touch.

    With the fourth stanza the myth comes abruptly to a halt.
Bacchylides, when he begins a mythical narrative, gets into
the swing of it and carries on until it is over; Pindar, less
predictable, likes to keep his auditors on their toes by the play
of aroused and foiled expectation. We saw him doing something similar in Nemean 3, also for an Aiginetan victor, where
he launched into an account of Herakles' doings only to stop
after a few lines declaring that he had sailed off course and
pausing to lay the ground for one of the island's myths. This
cannot be the explanation here, but the interesting lines in
which (we suppose) he explains what he is doing are difficult
and have been variously understood:

> To tell the whole long tale, art's bounds forbid
> and the hurrying hours. A spell
> tugs at my heart to join the new-moon rite.
> Although the deep sea has you by the waist,
> yet stand against its stratagems!

The bounds (more literally, law, usage) of epinician art do not of course really force Pindar to break off at this point; his myths vary considerably in length. This appeal to the laws of the genre is one of the ways of effecting a transition and is exactly paralleled by a passage in the first Isthmian where he is prevented by "the brief measure of the song" from recounting all the victor's triumphs. The new-moon rite which he longs to take part in is the actual celebration; he has promised to have the ode ready in time and is eager to fulfill the commission and give his victorious wrestler the praise he deserves. To do so, the poet has to turn wrestler himself, for he has to grapple with "the deep sea" which apparently prevents him from continuing the story of Telamon. What is this sea? On an initial reading there is no way of knowing, but a passage later on, the poem's next main transition, tells us. There (69 ff.), realizing that he cannot exhaust the abundance of Aiakid saga, the poet breaks off and turns directly to the victor and his clan. He does so by means of a nautical metaphor: "No passage beyond Cadiz! [Conventionally the limit of the known world.] Head your vessel back to Europe. I cannot go through the whole tale of the sons of Aiakos." The sea surely has the same sense in both passages—the abundance of Aiakid saga. The "stratagems" (more literally, plots) he must resist are most naturally understood as those of the sea, in the sense that the pressures, the sheer mass and magnificence of this narrative material, tempting him to continue with the adventures of Telamon, stand insidiously in the way of the task he longs to perform, to compose an ode praising the victor. The myth is ultimately only a means to this end, one of several, and there are other elements which the ode must include. It may be too that some other narrative from the annals of Aigina would suit the purposes of the ode better; he must not let himself be captured by Telamon.

This is admittedly curious stuff and Pindar is not usually

so convoluted. Or perhaps the difficulty is of our making—
we who read with knotted brows poems designed to give
delight. We have never attended the performance of a Pindaric ode and cannot picture the excitement and, yes, amuse-
ment of an audience of connoisseurs as they watch this
incredible man conjure up quite imaginary obstacles and
triumphantly circumvent them. But we must not pause, for
he is in full swing. Warming to his structural fiction, the wres-
tler-poet now confronts a different sort of obstacle:

> Plain to all you'll see
> how I win through in the light, my enemies
> outdone.

These enemies are now condensed into a single enemy, a
poetic rival, it seems:

> Let another, rancorous eyed,
> trundle his trite designs in darkness
> to fall stillborn.

This is not a particular poet whose identity could be uncovered by historical research (Bundy has mercifully rid the odes
of such phantoms) but again a purely imaginary figure, some
supposed local bard who fancies he could do the job better
or possibly a meanspirited person who resents the praise the
victor is receiving.

Stop smiling now, though, for with an abrupt change of
tone the poet draws himself up to his full height and declares:
"Whatever powers sovereign Destiny has granted me, I am
confident that onward time will bring them to the appointed
fulfillment." We assure ourselves anxiously nowadays that in
such passages Pindar—modest little man that he was—is not
referring to himself. The use of the first person singular in
the odes can admittedly be tricky (for some discussion see

chapter 1) and has been made more so by our overreaction against yesterday's critical errors which found the poet constantly intruding his own concerns into the fabric of a public poem. As a result we are reluctant to allow that Pindar often speaks out in the odes. To assert his powers, as he does here, is a way of telling the victor that he will receive the praise he deserves. It is the poet's word which grants the victor's act a luster and permanence it could not otherwise enjoy. There is something else too in these lordly verses which we should not hesitate to accept and enjoy, something that will be heard many times again in our several literatures, the poet's half impersonal pride in the art he serves and its ability to preserve against the tooth of time whatever is entrusted to its care.

At this point we feel a new surge of energy as, with a kind of ecstasy ("Weave sweetly, my lyre, now! weave this song too"), the poet returns to the world of Aiginetan myth. The story of Telamon gave him part of what he needed, but something more is required if his song is to perform its task perfectly. So he turns next to another even greater Aiakid hero, Peleus, but before doing so he puts the finishing touches to the Telamon story by speaking briefly of his two sons, Teukros who rules in distant Cyprus, and Aias lord of Salamis. He introduces the story of Peleus in the same way, via his son Achilles, his wife Thetis, and, at slightly greater length, finding room for a fine stretch of landscape, his grandson Neoptolemos (king of Epiros "where the pastoral headlands shelve down from Dodona to the sea"). He thus contrives to include a wide sweep of Aiginetan legend. Since he does the same thing in several other odes for Aiginetan victors (so too does Bacchylides in his thirteenth ode), it has been suggested that this may represent a particular feature of the epinician favored at Aigina which visiting poets were on the whole expected to observe. This may well be so, since it would have given the audience a proud sense of how rich their inheritance of saga was.

And now he is ready for Peleus. He tells his story in the customary way, juxtaposing three key moments, slightly out of chronological sequence, and suppressing the narrative links. The moment that concerns us is the final one, the marriage of Peleus and Thetis:

> Allmastering fire he foiled and the tearing claws
> of lions, their terrible teeth!
>
> to win his bride, the high-throned Nereid Thetis.
> And he saw them, seated about him,
> lords of sky and sea. They revealed
> their gifts, the power bred into the race.

In the full story Thetis transformed herself not only into fire and lion but also snake and water. The handbooks call her a goddess, but despite the grand way Pindar treats her she is rather the dangerous fairy bride of folklore who assumes these elemental shapes to resist capture by a mortal. By this marriage, a marriage divinely sanctioned and achieved by victory in a wrestling match (it all coheres!), the fierce natural powers which Thetis embodies are bred into the race of the Aiakidai and into all trueborn Aiginetans. *This,* we now see, is the moment Pindar has been heading for all along, this wrestler's marriage-victory won in the primal days when the ancestors lived out their turbulent lives in a world open to the presences from Olympos. Suddenly we understand (the poem's fiction is) why Pindar could not carry on the story of Telamon but had to look elsewhere, ranging through Aiakid legend until he came on what he was looking for, the seed or origin of the present victory, the foundational event which *made* the victor.

Armed with this knowledge, Pindar can now, in the last quarter of the poem, turn with full confidence to the victor and his clan. For the transition on which he turns, beautifully executed, he uses the nautical metaphor I have already discussed: the great ocean of Aiakid legend cannot be fully traversed, so he breaks off and completes the second lobe of the victory list. As part of his commission he was apparently required to work in an Isthmian victory won by his client's uncle, Kallikles, now dead, so he declares: "In his home by Akheron let him win the words that my tongue sounds, here where . . . he flowered with Corinthian garlands." Pindar has done what he was asked to do, but he knows that he cannot praise Kallikles adequately since, as he says, people speak best of what they themselves have seen. An eyewitness is needed and fortunately one is available, the victor's grandfather Euphanes, even though he too, we gather, is dead. The old man, Pindar says, "will gladly sing" the praise of Kallikles. Most editors print a past tense here, "he sang," and most translators follow them. The manuscript tradition, however, shows a future tense. The verb has been emended because the line as it stands does not scan and also, I suspect, because we do not understand how it can be said that a dead man *will* compose a song. The scholiast, however, did understand and can help us to enter into a kind of thinking remote from our own: "Euphanes will celebrate him, clearly as a dead man celebrating a dead man, showing that in Hades too there are those who admire outstanding people and that they possess the power of perception there." Perhaps we should remember in this context the story that in his last days Pindar had a dream in which Demeter, by another account Persephone, appeared and reproached him for the fact that she was the only deity he had never celebrated. He died a few days later but in his turn appeared to an old woman and dictated the required poem. Three words said to form part of this interesting composition have survived.

However the line is to be emended (it can be and has been), we should I believe keep the future tense, for the idea of poetry composed by the dead forms part of the design of this ode. In the second stanza we were told that the victor's father, were he still alive, *would have* sung the praise of his son and for several lines it appeared as though we were actually listening to that song. Now, at the end of the ode, we hear that the victor's dead grandfather *will* sing a song for another dead kinsman. And Pindar sticks to his conceit, if that is what it is, for it seems that the old man is entrusted with the poem's final task, a feature that sometimes formed part of an epinician commission, praise of the trainer, one Melesias. In pithy, idiomatic language drawn once again from wrestling, Pindar admiringly imagines how Euphanes would praise him: "Imitating Melesias, how he would turn this way and that as he fought, what a twist to his terms, a hard one to budge in the word game! A kindly friend to the good, for the black-hearted a tough man to face."

A conceit? Unless we are quite certain that Pindar's reality did not differ significantly from our own, we should be cautious about using such terms. In a beautiful passage from the fifth Pythian, written for the king of Libya, Pindar tells him how from their graves his royal ancestors "hear somehow with their enearthed minds as softly the offering of festal song falls like dew on his glory." Even so good a critic as Burton can speak of "the fantasy of the dead kings listening . . . to the hymns in praise of their posterity" (p. 144). Fantasy for us, yes, but perhaps not for Pindar, whose world was possessed of a sense of the unity of all being, a great vital continuum embracing divine, human, and natural, in which the dead, the living, and the unborn are bound more closely than we can imagine. How literally we are to take his words here it would be foolish to inquire; "somehow" (*poi*) shows that for Pindar too this is a mystery. At the same time we should not go to the other extreme and suppose that what we have here is no more than a literary device. In Pindar's world, the world of his poetry, the praising word which sounds here continues to sound there, granting the praised act a duration it could not otherwise achieve. Hence when he speaks in the prelude of tongue drawing up the word from deep mind by gift of the Graces (goddesses of Earth's nurturing powers), he may mean something more than the poet's deepest meditation. He may be thinking too of the enearthed minds of the dead, those *pères profonds* who share our joys and in their mysterious way can give them a longer life.

Isthmian 8: A Myth and Its Occasion

No other ode starts so abruptly. Written for an Aiginetan boy called Kleandros who had won the pankration, Isthmian 8 lacks the customary prelude and opens with the poet simply calling on Kleandros' companions to begin the celebration in front of his father's house. We might expect that it would be the poet who led or initiated the ceremony and are surprised by the way he seems to dissociate himself from it. "I too," he says, "though sick at heart, am bidden to invoke the golden Muse." Still more surprising and indeed unparalleled in the odes is the accent of grief running through the first stanza. "Freed from great sorrows, let us not go bereft of garlands," the poet declares. "Do not brood on your troubles. Let us dwell no more on unmanageable ills but give public utterance to some glad strain even after our trials." For deliverance has finally come:

> The stone of Tantalos poised above our heads
> some god has turned aside,
> too heavy a burden for Hellas.

This danger threatening the whole of Greece can only be the Persian invasion, most probably that of 480–79, and the lines make clear that it has passed very recently. The poem must have been written a year or so after, perhaps for the Isthmian festival of 478. But the danger has passed, Greece has emerged victorious, and at Salamis the Aiginetan naval forces covered themselves with glory. Why then the note of persisting sadness which the poet finds so difficult to shake off? A great victory should be the occasion for joy—whatever the casualties; a resolute people accepts them as the inevitable price to be paid. And even if, as the scholiast suggests, the victor lost relatives in the fighting—probable enough, though the text says nothing about it—this still does not fully account for the sorrowful tone of the lines. The explanation, it has been thought, is to be found in the poet's own situation. Thebes had disgraced herself in the war by throwing in her lot with the enemy, at Plataia (479) actually fighting on the Persian side, and as a Theban Pindar is deeply ashamed of his city's conduct. "Writing immediately after the Persian War," Bowra says, "Pindar is still haunted by it and is impelled to speak at the start about his own feelings . . ." (*Pindar*, 330).

Needless to say, so bluntly autobiographical a reading is not found acceptable today, and indeed it is hard to be comfortable with it. Pindar had after all undertaken to write a poem celebrating a victory in the games and it is scarcely credible that he would see fit to mar the happy occasion by announcing that he personally feels terrible. Why then does he begin by saying that he is sick at heart? A clever interpretation which puts this embarrassing cri de coeur in a decent epinician light was proposed some years ago by Carl Ruck in an article in *Hermes* 96 (1968). If the poet describes himself as "overwhelmed with sorrow," it is because he has "assumed his patron's grief." Kleandros, the young victor, is grieving for the death of a relative. True, nothing is said about this sad loss here, but if we turn to the conclusion of the poem it may be that we find what we are looking for. There, before uttering the final words in praise of the victor, Pindar praises a dead cousin, Nikokles, "perhaps killed in the war," Ruck suggests, taking his cue from the scholiast. The poet thus has a double commission, to celebrate Kleandros' athletic triumph and to mourn with him for the death of a brave relative. This interpretation is supported by the myth, which in its powerful final section, centered on Achilles, describes his heroic valor at Troy and tells how his death in battle was mourned by the Muses themselves. "Nikokles, then, who fought to throw off the stone of Tantalos and to win freedom," Ruck writes, "has as his mythic prototype Achilles' epic life and honored death. Nikokles' own death receives not only its dirge but its memorial for his actions and its redemption in the release from sorrow occasioned by the young Kleandros' celebration."

This would give us a finely constructed epinician poem and one can only regret that Pindar did not see his way to composing it. Unfortunately, the poem he did compose fails to provide a piece of information which is indispensable to Ruck's reading: *it says nothing about Nikokles' death in battle.* He is praised handsomely and at length, but he is praised solely as an athlete. Pindar turns to him immediately after the myth:

And this holds good today. See where it comes,
the chariot of the Muses hastening to proclaim

the memory of Níkokles the boxer.

Honor this man!
who in the Isthmian valley
assumed the Dorian garland.
For he too in his day
knocked down every boxer in the region,
routed them all. No escaping those fists.

This was the place to work in the man's crowning glory and announce that in battle he proved a no less formidable foe to the Persians. As other odes show, there was no problem about mentioning the death in war of relatives of the victor.* But nothing is said on this score and it is surely inconceivable that a poem which began by speaking of Greece's deliverance from the agony of war should end by praising a man who gave his life to bring that deliverance about and then fail to mention the fact.

Reluctantly we have to abandon the critic's poem and see what we can make of the poet's. We must ask again why Pindar announces that he is heartsick and why he speaks of Greece's great victory in such dispirited terms. We can no longer say that his grief is an epinician fiction assumed for the sake of his patron, for even if Kleandros was overwhelmed with sorrow for his cousin's death, that can hardly be at issue in this passage filled with thoughts of the peril just passed since the man did not meet his death fighting to avert that peril. However, if we hope for the right answer to our question, we must be careful to ask that question in the right way. We should not ask why Pindar the Theban feels heartsick but why Pindar the poet tells us about his feelings

*"On a single day, war's harsh snowstorm robbed the happy hearth of four men," Isthmian 4.17 f. In Isthmian 7.24 f. it is said that the victor "gave his uncle a share of his garland, he to whom the wargod brought the fate of death."

at the start of an epinician ode. And perhaps we should also ask why this ode lacks the usual prelude and why the poet seems to dissociate himself from the chorus. What may prove to be at issue here is the crucial epinician bond between victor and poet, whereby the poet, as the victor's guest-friend, visits his city eager to give him the praise he deserves. Coming from a city which disgraced itself in the war to one which fought magnificently, he does not feel able to open with some brilliant festive image or to join directly in the celebration of an Aiginetan victor. There is no need to suppose that this is merely an epinician fiction. Pindar's odes were written and performed in historical time and place, not in the sealed generic vacuum within which recent critical dogma has sought to encapsulate them. We have here, I suggest, another example of what we saw the poet doing in Nemean 3 and will see him doing at greater length in Nemean 7, accepting or taking advantage of a real situation and at once bringing it within the compass of epinician convention.

For in the lines that soon follow, Pindar goes on to do what he regularly does, state his poetic credentials, but this time he has to do so with unusual deliberation. Elsewhere in the Aiginetan odes the special relation between Thebes and Aigina can be taken almost for granted; in Nemean 4, for example, it can simply be said of an Aiginetan who won in the Theban games that the citizens wreathed him with flowers "for Aigina's sake." Here, the old bond must be rebuilt from the ground up:

A man bred in Thebes of the Seven Gates
must pay Aigína's tribute of faultless song.
There were two of them born of one father,
Theba, Aigína,
and found favor in the eyes of Zeus.

> To one he gave a home
>> by the lovely waters of Dirka,
> mistress of a city of horsemen.
> But you, Aigína, he brought
>> to Vineland and the bed of love
> where you bore him Aíakos, dearest of mortal men.

(Vineland was the old name of Aigina.) Whatever political differences may have arisen between the two cities, the traditional friendship is strong enough to make a Theban poet uniquely qualified to praise an Aiginetan victor.

The passage leads by an easy transition to the next regular feature, celebration of the victor's homeland which takes the familiar form of some lines in honor of the Aiakidai. We hear of their surpassing qualities, their bravery in war and their wisdom, but there is one novel item. Of Aiakos the founding father it is said that "he settled disputes even among the gods." Aiakos was commonly represented as the judge of mortals in the next world, but nowhere else is he credited with this far higher judicial office. The story seems to be Pindar's invention, devised to introduce the myth, also apparently his invention, which tells of just such a dispute, the solution of which depends on a man of exceptional virtue being found. It is I think a structural flaw, by no means a fatal one but still a flaw, that while this virtuous man proves to be a son of Aiakos, Aiakos himself has no hand in settling the dispute. But let us see what happens.

The two greatest powers on Olympos, Zeus and Poseidon, were competing for the hand of the sea goddess Thetis. Strife was avoided by the intervention of Themis, Ordonnance, an august if shadowy personage out of Hesiod, who warned the assembled gods that were Thetis to be joined to either Zeus or Poseidon she would bear a son mightier than the father, wielding a weapon more potent than the thunderbolt or the trident. (Does Pindar for a moment contemplate something like the brave eschatology of the Norseman who knew that the supreme power in the universe would not always be supreme?) To avert the birth of a being who would disrupt the order of heaven, Themis tells them, they must give up their pursuit of Thetis. Instead:

> Let her lie with a mortal man
> and see her son dead in battle,
>> though his hands are heavy as Ares,
>> bolt lightning his feet.

Her advice is that Thetis be married to Peleus, a supremely virtuous man. The gods approve her counsel and the marriage duly takes place:

> Her words
> fell on good soil and fruited richly.

For the son born to Thetis and Peleus was Achilles, and to describe his career there follows a furious passage driven forward as though at a single breath by a series of violent or unusual verbs, the clauses mostly linked by the lightest of Greek connectives:

> He dyed Mysia's green vineyards black
>> with the blood of Télephos,
> bridged the Atreidai home, set Helen free,
> hacked out the thews of Troy, whoever tried to stop
>> him
> marshaling battle's murderous work across the plain,
> Memnon that tough fighter, Hector, all Troy's best—
> Achilles pointed them the way to death
> and showed forth his root in Aigína.

Achilles' actions are presented in a light that to readers of the
Iliad at least is unfamiliar. (It looks as though Pindar is drawing here on the lost Troy epic the *Aithiopis*.) He is shown not
simply as the greatest Greek hero but as a savior, freeing
Helen, ensuring a passage home for the Atreidai, and single-
handedly routing the enemy. And his death is no less triumphant, for even then glory did not desert him. The Muses
stood around his funeral pyre as they delivered their antiphonal lament:

> So great a man that even dead
> the immortals judged it right
> to give him to the Muses for their singing.

This unusual myth is taken to be Pindar's. Given the fluid
nature of Greek mythology and the fact that so much of it can
never have been recorded, it is normally unwise to make such
a claim, but this story of strife in heaven averted by letting a
goddess taste the human pain of death does not look like a
product of the folk imagination and it may well be that Pindar
invented it for the present poem. If so, we need to ask why.
The primary purpose of this, as of all other myths in the odes,
must be to praise the victor and his community and to show
how victory came about, the ground from which it grew. For
this, however, any story about Achilles would suffice; with
such an ancestor, how should an Aiginetan athlete not prevail? Why then *this* story, with its portentous Olympian setting? The explanation can only be that the poet was required
or wished to include a number of different themes and knew
of no existing myth which could be made to apply to them
all. In addition to his primary encomiastic task, he must pay
tribute to a dead relative, also an athlete. Not in itself an
unusual feature; we found the same thing in Nemean 4.

Third, either part of the commission or judged by the poet to be fitting, he must build in as background the recent war, Aigina's achievements in that war an earnest of the victor's achievement today, her losses there acting as the dark reverse of today's brightness and by the end giving way to and overcome by that brightness. A fourth and more dubious element—so let it hang loose for the moment—may be that something more had to be said about the theme with which the poem began, the doubtful standing in Aigina at the present time of a Theban poet and his questionable right to celebrate an Aiginetan victor.

A difficult commission. We begin to see why Pindar had to come up with a myth of his own that could embrace and illuminate these various themes. How does his myth perform its task? It tells two great and potentially disastrous stories, the one proceeding from the other, in both of which an Aiginetan played a central role. War in heaven was averted by the marriage of Thetis to the Aiginetan Peleus, a marriage which led to the birth of Achilles. In the archetypal earthly war at Troy, Achilles is presented in the light of a savior, and the poet ends by declaring that by his actions "he showed forth his root in Aigina." Rooted in that noble soil, Kleandros inevitably triumphed in the Isthmian games. The myth ends with the picture of the Muses standing by Achilles' pyre to deliver the praise which makes his name immortal. With the assertion "and this holds good today," the poet passes to the similar honor which they bestow on the dead boxer, Nikokles. Similar, yes, but it has to be granted that there would be a more perfect consonance between the myth and its occasion if Nikokles, like Achilles, had fallen in battle. We must be content with the poem Pindar wrote, however, and say that Achilles' career, in life as in death, is the foundational event which underlies and makes possible Aiginetan *virtù* of every kind. It serves as a means of praising all her noble dead, those who fought and died in the recent war and those who like Nikokles glorified the island by their performance in the virile arts of peace.

What of the fourth theme on which the myth may also have to throw its light? At whatever cost to today's critical principles, I believe that we must grant the poet's situation a place in the ode's plot and accept that in speaking of the war in a way that seems inappropriate to a glorious victory he is speaking for himself not for his patron. We need not believe that Pindar's personal feelings are expressed here and may, if we so wish, take everything in a purely epinician light. As a Theban Pindar cannot fully share the joy felt by his hosts at the recent military victory and is doubtful about his right to celebrate the present athletic victory of his Aiginetan patron. His city's shame has alienated him from his audience, and this alienation (suggested by the opening lines where the poet separates himself from the chorus and probably made visible in performance) must be overcome before he can carry out his epinician task. Pindar justifies his presence first, as we saw, by carefully reknitting the old bond between Thebes and Aigina, then by creating a myth so vast in its implications that the differences between one Greek city and another fade into insignificance. As a human being he can rejoice with other members of our species that war in heaven was averted; as a Greek he can join with all other Greeks in celebrating the heroic life of Achilles, honoring his bravery in the archetypal war at Troy and mourning his death there.

This myth, even if we feel that it does not fit its occasion quite perfectly, is still a notable invention. Does it, perhaps, go beyond its occasion? I am thinking of the words spoken by Themis:

Let her lie with a mortal man
and see her son dead in battle.

Bury called this one of Pindar's "happiest and deepest criti-
cisms on life," apparently taking it as a way of pointing the
contrast between our mortality and the immortal life of the
gods. These lines, however, do not simply say that the goddess must marry a mortal man and bear a mortal son, but
that this son must die in war. It seems as though Achilles'
death is in some sense a sacrificial death: as though potential
turbulence in heaven can be forestalled only by unleashing
an almost comparable turbulence on earth, as though the
price of concord among the gods, the one means of averting
the disruption of the cosmic order of things, is the birth and
death of a man whose powers, almost akin to those of the
immortals, threaten the earthly order of things by crossing
the line that keeps mortal man mortal. Is this a way of claiming, in the myth's grand terms, that those who died heroically
in the Persian War died that Greece might live? I suspect that
Pindar may be saying something more than this but I do not
know what it is.

Nemean 7: Truth and the Measure of Praise

Almost all poetry is occasional in some sort, but the occasions vary greatly and this leads to different kinds of
poems. "On Beginning the Study of Anglo-Saxon Grammar"
is an occasional poem, so is Lycidas. The difference is that no
lively train of conventional responses springs up to greet the
subject of the Borges poem, and no preexisting form stands
ready to accommodate his thoughts about this project,
whereas Milton could count on a wide range of feelings being
aroused by the fact of a young life abruptly cut short, its

promise unfulfilled. More important, both Milton and his
public possessed an established, prestigious form, the pastoral elegy, to house this sad occasion. Pindar's epinicians also
have their form, a stricter form than Milton's, and their occasion: a more predictable one—talented people do not regularly die young, while the games produced their steady crop
of victors—and, in our eyes at least, a more restricted one.
The question is or perhaps should be: *how* restricted? How far
can the occasion of victory be stretched, what may its poem
include beyond the matter immediately at hand? Schooled by
Bundy (the epinician ode is "dedicated to the single purpose
of eulogizing men and communities"), many now incline to
say, very little. One may wonder if this can really be so. Pindar, after all, is the name of a poet, not of the process whereby
victory odes were produced. And Pindar and his victors did
not exist within a vacuum called epinician poetry but in the
big blooming buzzing confusion called life where unexpected,
untoward things do happen and demand attention. Can we
be sure that a good deal of obdurate external circumstance
did not find its way into these poems? This may sound like a
call to bring back the biographical, historical matter which
Bundy's razor has shorn away, and in so doing lose sight of
what it gave us, our new understanding of the highly disciplined form in which Pindar worked. And yet the razor may
have cut too deep. I do not mean simply that it has diminished
the human range, the sheer interest, of Pindar's poetry. Par-
adoxically, it may also have left us with less reason to admire
its formal accomplishment. To dispose the fact of victory and
what went with it within the strict compass of the epinician;
to do this one thing again and again and each time seem to
be doing something new: that certainly is a formidable
achievement. It is surely a still greater achievement to admit
into an ode "the untutored incident which actually occurred,"

in Kipling's phrase, and which, while it may have had nothing immediately to do with the victory, would have been in the minds of victor and community, and do this *without impairing the integrity of the form.* Nemean 7 may be a work of this latter sort.

It was written for an Aiginetan boy called Sogenes who had won the pentathlon (footrace, long jump, throwing the discus and javelin, wrestling). There are two myths. The first, briefer one is about Aias and begins by contrasting this underpraised hero (as Pindar saw him) with a man who is said to have been overpraised, Odysseus. We then hear how Aias sailed to Troy and there, after the war he had done so much to win, committed suicide when the armor of Achilles was awarded to Odysseus rather than to him. This is followed by a longer story about another Aiginetan hero, Achilles' son Neoptolemos, who after the sack of Troy was killed at Delphi and granted heroic honors there. The scholia to this poem preserve from Alexandrian learning the information that Pindar had offended the Aiginetans by the account he had given of Neoptolemos' death in a previous poem and that in Nemean 7 he made amends by coming up with a more favorable version. This piece of information was accepted by most earlier critics and seemed to receive its full confirmation in 1908 with the publication of a papyrus containing sizable portions of the earlier poem (paian 6). There we read that during the sack of Troy Neoptolemos killed the aged Priam at the altar of his hearth, whereupon Apollo vowed that he would never return home, and himself killed Neoptolemos at Delphi "as he was fighting with the temple servants about the honors due to him." An ignominious end for the son of the greatest of heroes. Since the story Nemean 7 tells about Neoptolemos is different in some important respects and portrays him in a decidedly better light—there is no mention of his impious

killing of Priam, and his own death at Delphi is due not to
Apollo but to what looks more like an accident—the Alexandrian lead was accepted with renewed confidence and the
ode was read as the poet's apologia. *Enfin Bundy vint* and,
pronouncing Nemean 7 "a straightforward enkomion," dis-
missed what had become the standard account in a contemp-
tuous sentence (I.4). Although Bundy's view of the matter
has not altogether carried the day, it has been sufficiently
influential to fuel a continuing controversy which is doing
some damage to a magnificent poem. The best course is to
clear our minds and listen to the work itself.

Pindar begins in his weightiest manner by invoking the
birth goddess Eleithuia, "enthroned beside the deep-minded
Fates," who brings us by our severally allotted paths through
the succession of nights and days to the season of bright-
limbed Youth. Then—one imagines the dancers pausing for
a moment and turning to the young hero of the hour—from
this picture of the whole human condition a particular life
stands out in sharp relief: *Sogenes,* son of *Thearion,* victor in
the pentathlon, from Aigina—but for the final element, direct
statement gives way to periphrasis: "He lives in a city which
loves the danced poem, home of the Aiakidai of the clashing
spears." Music and war, sweetness conjoined with violence,
as so often in odes for Aigina. Pindar next launches into a
grand formulation of one of his most cherished themes, poetry's power to preserve whatever is entrusted to it:

> Who hits his form and wins
> > casts a delectable theme
> into the running water of the Muses.
> But should our greatness lack its poem—
> > the big dark takes it.
> For fine things done we know this mirror only:

if Memory who wears the glistering crown
grants them the echoing verses that are toil's return.

"I prefer a poet who thinks," Nietzsche said, with Pindar
in mind. In the discursive lines that follow, Pindar is thinking
but not in the way we do, the way Athens was starting to
teach the world to think. His is the archaic mode of thought,
pithy, sententious, proverbial, preferring a picture to bare
statement, asserting rather than proving, and seeming to
jump abruptly from assertion to assertion. The passage begins:

Wise men know that the third wind will come,
they are not hurt by greed:
Poor, rich, alike must go
to death's mark. . . .

Did the Aiginetans catch the drift straight off? Seafaring people, they would no doubt have seen that the wise men are
weather-wise, skippers who know that today's fair wind will
not last and set sail at once rather than wait for tomorrow's
chance of a fatter cargo. Why the *third* wind? The next sentence ("Poor, rich . . ."), coming with no connecting link, provides the explanation: the third wind rouses the proverbially
fatal third *wave* which no swimmer or ship can climb. A culture sharing a common fund of experience would have had
no trouble with this terse, elliptic thinking, even if we
groundlings from a splintered world must grope our way.
Clear enough, then, and bearing clearly enough on the lines
about poetry just before: the victor and his family know that
the big dark is coming on their triumph as surely as the third
wave and are not "hurt by greed" (literally gain, desire for
gain), that is, they are not niggardly about engaging a poet
to ward it off, whatever the expense. Few in the audience

would have been so low-minded as to take Pindar to be referring to his fee. The bond between victory and victory
poem, between victor and poet, must be sealed by the grace
of the welcome, the honor accorded to the visitor at the feast
accompanying the celebration, and the treasured gift he takes
away with him when he leaves. (No doubt there was some
shrewd Mediterranean bargaining about the poet's honorar-
ium, but that is the prose of the matter and has no place in
the song.)

What follows would perhaps have proved more puzzling:

> . . . I think the tale of Odysseus
> greater than the toils he suffered
> thanks to the lovely voice of Homer.

> For on his falsehoods and the cunning of his winged
>   words
> an awesome power lies. Speech-skill
> deceives the mind with tales. The many
> are blind at heart. Could they have seen the truth,
> never would Aias, angry for the arms denied him,
> have slid the sword through his chest—Aias,
> the best in battle they had next to Achilles.

And two highly energetic lines tell how Aias went with the
great armada to Troy to recover Helen. Then the literal sea
on which he sails turns back to metaphor and becomes the
wave of death, and darkly the movement which began with
birth and bright youth and athletic triumph and the faith in
poetry's saving strength ends with this, the death wave which
falls on all alike, illustrious and obscure. To suggest the power
of these lines (and to color the poor English words standing
in for them with the accent of great poetry), it may help to

draw on a roughly comparable passage from our own tradition:

> Fame is the spur that the clear spirit doth raise
> (That last infirmity of Noble mind)
> To scorn delights and live laborious dayes;
> But the fair Guerdon when we hope to find,
> And think to burst out into sudden blaze,
> Comes the blind Fury with th' abhorred shears,
> And slits the thin spun life. (*Lycidas*, 70–76)

Poetry, then, our one means of escaping the big dark, cannot
be trusted; "inset with glittering falsehoods," as Pindar says
in another ode where he speaks of language's ambiguous
powers (Olympian 1.29), it may deceive the mass of mankind.
Power indeed it has; thanks to poetry, Odysseus's story is
known everywhere, but the story is not altogether true. Homer overpraised him, showing him in too favorable colors.
Worse still, another, greater man, Aias, has been underpraised. Odysseus, gifted with a speech-skill akin to the
poet's ("You told your tale skillfully, like a bard," Alkinoos
says to him in the *Odyssey*, 11.368), deceived the crowd and
won for himself the prize which by rights should have gone
to Aias. And poetry did nothing to set the record straight,
leaving posterity with the story of Aias' dishonored death.
Worst of all, it seems that even the most truthful poetry af-
fords no protection against the third great wave which breaks
impartially on all we are and all we do.

Immediately after the lines I quoted from *Lycidas*, Milton
turns to a different kind of fame. ("Fame is no plant that
grows on mortal soil, / Nor in the glistering foil / Set off to th'
world, nor in broad rumour lies, / But lives and spreds aloft
by those pure eyes, / And perfet witnes of all judging Jove.")
Pindar does very much the same thing, doing it through

myth, always the medium for his strongest thinking. As the
second movement of the ode begins, he turns to the other
Aiginetan hero, Neoptolemos, whose career, like that of Aias,
was checkered and who, again like Aias, had perhaps been
misrepresented or underpraised by a poet:

> But honor is theirs
> whose fame, when they are dead,
> God swells and ripens.
>   And so to earth's great navel-stone I went
> bringing my aid. In Delphi's holy ground
> Neoptólemos lies.

Whereas the fame granted by poetry is uncertain, honor
granted by God lives on, and it is this honor which Pindar
here claims for Neoptolemos. It is not in the poet's gift, yet
the poet can tend it and this is what Pindar proceeds to do,
declaring (text uncertain, I follow what seems the likeliest
reading) that he himself went to Delphi—where the hero met
his questionable end—"bringing aid." Why does Pindar tell
us about this visit? The Pythian games were held at Delphi,
but it is a Nemean victory he is celebrating, so he did not go
there to watch Sogenes perform. He might well have gone
there for the paian which was written for the Delphians, but
he can hardly claim that he brought aid to Neoptolemos' reputation in that poem. It looks as though he is referring to the
present poem. He says that he went or has gone to Delphi to
bring aid—that is, surely, to correct the damaging story, which
he himself had narrated, that Neoptolemos was killed there
by Apollo—in the sense that he is about to describe a journey
culminating at Delphi which will show the hero's death in a
far more favorable light. Pindar, then, is doing here what we
see him doing several times in the odes, presenting a new
development in the poem he is writing as an action under-

taken by himself. "Quickly, Phintis," he says to the driver of
the victor's mule team in the sixth Olympian. "We must set
out on a clear road and come to the source of these men's
race," he goes on, announcing a journey to places where the
events the poem is about to describe took place. In Nemean 7
the announcement of the poet's trip to Delphi introduces an
account of how Neoptolemos set out from Troy after the sack
on a voyage that may have been ill-starred in some respects
but ended honorably, at Delphi. Heading first for the Aegean
island of Skyros where he was born, he missed it and came
instead to Epiros, the coastal region of northwest Greece.
There he ruled as king—for a short time, though his descendants still hold the kingship. Finally he came to Delphi to
bring the firstfruits of his Trojan victory (a pious act), but once
again misfortune overtook him: "In a quarrel over meats he
was stabbed by a man with a knife." Or apparent misfortune,
for although this looks like a dusty sort of death, better die
this way than as a sinner at the hands of the god. Moreover,
from this point on Neoptolemos gains rapidly in stature:

> Greatly his Delphic hosts were grieved.
> But it was fate's due he paid. It had to be
> that there, within the ancient grove
> one of the royal Aiákidai
> should dwell forever by God's walled house
> to watch due order kept
> when they sacrifice to the Heroes
>   as beasts are led to the altar.

In life Neoptolemos may have been an ambiguous figure, but
respice finem: abused, misrepresented, the dead hero lying in
this holy soil has been redeemed and is now a transfigured,
awful presence.

The myth, its task accomplished, is over and we feel the

usual quickening of pace as Pindar prepares for the final transition to the third movement of the ode:

> For Justice of the fair name three words suffice:
> No false witness presides over the deeds
> of your sons, Aigína, and the sons of Zeus.

On the face of it, these lines refer to Neoptolemos. He will be
at Delphi, from his tomb bearing witness to any deeds that
Aiginetan athletes may henceforth perform there. But we expect something more specifically relevant to the present context, and since the question of poetic truth is a central concern
of this ode, poetry's power to bear *true* witness, we had best
take the poet to be referring to himself (his myth has dealt
justly with Neoptolemos and no more need be said), the more
so in view of the difficult passage which follows. "I am em-
boldened to say this," Pindar declares, then pauses at the end
of the strophe, making us wait for what he has to announce
until the chorus begins the new movement of the antistrophe:
"a path of words at home empowered for brilliant actions."
The poet possesses these words "at home," that is, by virtue
of his poetic gift which empowers him to speak of brilliant
actions—those of the victor, to whom he is about to return.
The words have been granted or revealed to him by the actions of Neoptolemos which he has just been narrating, actions in no way discreditable but, properly understood,
glorious, and foundational for the victory he is celebrating.
The lines, then, however exactly they should be translated,
are transitional and are at once followed by a conventional
indication of a new theme to come: "Enough! for rest is sweet
in every task. There is surfeit even of honey and the flowers
of Aphrodite." With this, the poet does what we expect him
to do and directs his attention to the victor.

    This section is the least predictable area of an ode and

may contain—in addition to renewed praise, the poet's relation to his client, poetry's power to ensure fame, and the
victory list—sometimes the second part of the victory list,
prayers for the future, and other less constant elements (a few
words in praise of the trainer may, for instance, be required).
Some of the expected features are found here, but the section
is unusually long and most critics have found it difficult.
Those who read Nemean 7 as the poet's personal apologia
see him struggling to talk his way out of a difficult situation.
My own reading of the passage is different, though I do believe that we are expected to have the troublesome business
of Neoptolemos in mind and that the poem is enriched if we
have it in mind. For the poet, a virtuoso delighting in his
consummate virtuosity and addressing connoisseurs of the
epinician art, takes advantage of it and builds it into his fabric
of praise.

Pindar begins, conventionally enough, by addressing the
victor's father Thearion, who appeared briefly at the start of
the ode, reintroducing him by rephrasing the initial topos
about the different paths of life allotted to us. He goes on: "I
am here as guest-friend (*xeinos*). Warding off dark censure,
as though leading streams of water to the man I love, I will
sing true praise of his glory." Of the pastoral images in *Lycidas*
Rosemund Tuve remarked that "time had got them ready to
mean all that Milton was able to say." One might make the
same observation of a passage like this. It bears closely on the
present poem but reaches beyond it, into the rest of the odes,
and belongs, we must suppose, to the inherited speech of
praise poetry. In speaking of himself as guest-friend, Pindar
is appealing to the concept or rather the bond of *xenia*, the
relationship which binds poet to victor not as paid celebrant
but as friend visiting friend and eager to please him. Xenia is
central to the epinician poet's art and especially important to

this ode if there was a suspicion in Aigina that Pindar had spoken of one of their heroes in a way that a friend should not speak. We have come across the root of this word already in the line about the distress felt by Neoptolemos' Delphic hosts (*xenagetai*) at his death, and we will hear it three times more. As *xeinos* Pindar says that he wards off dark censure. Who, we wonder, is likely to censure the victor and his family at such a time? And why trouble to say that censure is dark (*skoteinos*)? The questions are worth pursuing in a certain detail, since both noun and adjective belong to an epinician semantic field with lines of force ramifying through the odes.*

Censure, or blame, is dark because it consigns an action or person to oblivion (*lēthē*, or *latha* in Pindar's poetic dialect). The big dark (*skotos polus*) which waits for all fine achievement can be countered only by the sounding word of praise, blame's bright reverse, which bestows on achievement the prestige of appearance, making it radiantly visible. Pindar has many ways of expressing this. The victor, he says, is "set aflame" by the Muses (Isthmian 7.23) or by "the clamor of the Graces" (Nemean 6.38), fostering spirits of victory song; the poet, praying that "the pure light of the clamorous Graces" may not fail him, declares that the victor has "escaped helpless silence" (Pythian 9.89 ff.). Rather more complexly, he speaks of the "unknown silences" ("le silence et l'oubli," as the Budé translation has it) awaiting those who make no venture, while even for those who do venture there is, literally, a nonappearance (*aphaneia*) of good fortune before they reach their goal (Isthmian 4.30 ff.). Over every action, as it strives for the grace of appearance, hangs the danger of falling into the dis-grace of nonappearance.†

*I am indebted in what follows to Marcel Detienne's *Les maîtres de vérité dans la Grèce archaïque* (1967), especially chapters 2, 3, and 4.

†The lexicon, referring to this passage, renders aphaneia as "obscurity, uncertainty," so too Slater, which leave us merely with the banal observation that one can't tell how things will turn out. The legend of Pindar as a poet who does not think is maintained by refusing to take his words seriously.

In the present poem Pindar uses the image of the mirror which poetry holds up to great actions, without which, as the scholiast glosses, they would become invisible, nonapparent (*aphaneis*). The image speaks of poetry's power to grant visibility, but poetry also grants duration ("the word lives longer than the act, whatever by gift of the Muses tongue draws up from deep mind," Nemean 4.6 ff.). Poetry is the gift of the Muses who are the daughters of Memory, Mnamosuna, and "the Muse loves to remember great contests" (Nemean 1.11 f.). It is by virtue of this memorializing power that fine actions escape the darkness and oblivion that would otherwise overwhelm them ("But ancient glory sleeps and men forget whatever is not joined to streams of verse and comes not to the perfect flower of speech," Isthmian 7.16 ff.). Poetry possesses this power because it sees into the truth of things (*alatheia*), the truth that, had men seen it (*idemen*, Nemean 7.25), would have saved great Aias from his dishonored death and from the latha, oblivion, that in another poem is said to have taken hold of him (Nemean 8.24).

The defense against latha is alatheia, "truth." This word, in Pindar, is coming to acquire its later sense, our sense, of correctness, conformity to an objective standard or reality, whereby it is opposed to falsehood. Against the falsehoods (*pseudea*) which Homer promulgated about Odysseus, Pindar sets the truth, alatheia, about Aias which should have prevailed but did not, and the true or not-false witness (*ou pseudis*) which he himself bears to another misrepresented hero, Neoptolemos. But Pindar's alatheia still retains the older sense which is opposed not so much to falsehood as to latha, the darkness of oblivion. The poet who speaks true saves the victor's triumph from the big dark and by holding up the mirror of Memory to it makes it shine through the centuries.

The poet can also make it grow, for growth too belongs to this same semantic field. We are not yet done with these

lines of Nemean 7. There is a saying, Pindar tells us, that a
fine action should not be hidden silently in the earth
(Nemean 9.6 f.). At the negative pole, this is equivalent to
censuring or blaming it. But the silent earth may also be seen
positively, as the region from which things grow into the light
and become visible. At the end of Olympian 7 Pindar says
"Do not hide the seed of this family"—do not, that is, censure
it by consigning it to darkness. But at once, since "seed"
implies growth, negative turns positive and the family seed
rises into the light of praise. As Pindar's language says for
him, the praising speech he inherited and enriched by his
genius: "with the kharites of this family, the city too has
thaliai." Uncapitalized, as our texts, following the modern
typographical convention, print the word, kharites supposedly
means the glory or joy of victory, and thaliai means festivity,
so that the sense is: "With the victory joy of this family, the
city too enjoys a holiday." But our typographical convention
is not Greek and a Greek would have heard the Kharites or
Graces here too, and in thaliai he would have heard the verb
thallein, to flourish or flower, and also Thalia, the name of one
of the Graces, so that what Pindar's words are really saying
is that thanks to the Graces the whole city is not simply enjoying a holiday but is flowering, blossoming. As the servant
and minister of the Graces, it is the poet's task to assist this
process, to help this *floraison* take place. He comes with them
to the victor (Isthmian 5.21), he tends their garden (Olympian
9.27), and it is as gardener that we see him in Nemean 7,
guiding streams of water to the man he loves. We are told in
a number of passages that for us are metaphoric but may for
the poet be nearly literal that song waters the roots of the city
or family tree. The image here, as the scholiast saw, is that of
a man irrigating a garden. Water-bringer, gardener, the poet
wards off dark censure and brings true praise.

There is still one further point to notice briefly about
these lines, one belonging primarily to the imagery and structure of the present poem, and that is the role which water
plays. We came across it first as the victor cast his theme "into
the running waters of the Muses," thereby setting in motion
a process which could save his victory from oblivion. Water
then became a negative, destructive force, the disastrous third
wave which eventually falls on us all. Here, it is a saving,
fostering power once more, the water with which the praising
poet tends the glory of the victor or perhaps of his father.
(We may again recall *Lycidas* where the "whelming tide" is
transformed into the waves over which Christ safely walked.)

The true praise he brings is the reverse of the censure he
wards off. The relation, at once antithetical and complemen-
tary, between praise and blame is traditional in older Greek
thinking as in that of other archaic societies and can assume
different forms. In the passage which follows, Pindar takes a
seemingly mild form of blame which can yet prove deadly,
underpraise, and sets it against the exaggerated praise or
overpraise which may damage the recipient by arousing men's
envy and resentment. Odysseus, as we saw, was overpraised,
Aias underpraised; Neoptolemos too was underpraised until
Pindar finally set the record straight and bore true witness to
his heroic status. What of the young hero of the hour, Sogenes—how is he to be praised? Will his celebrant be able to
avoid the perils of deficient and excessive praise which press
threateningly against the mean or measure of true praise?
This predicament, an agonizing one as Pindar presents it in
a brilliant fiction, is exactly expressed by the chorus in the
Agamemnon as they ask themselves how they should salute
their victorious master on his return from Troy: "How am I
to address you, how pay you homage, neither overshooting
the mark nor falling short of the true measure of joy?" (785 ff.)

Pindar nowhere formulates this distinction so explicitly, though he alludes to it several times (in Pythian 1.42 ff., for example, by means of an athletic metaphor), but we find similar statements elsewhere in Greek literature, and it fits in well with everything we know of the Greek habit of thinking in polar opposites. (A son burying his father, Plato says, must not let the ceremony exceed the customary dignity nor fall short of the honor traditionally paid to the dead, *Laws* 717d.) It is at all events in terms of this distinction that Pindar proceeds to conduct an elaborate debate with himself as he ponders the problem of taking the difficult middle way between the two types of faulty praise. By showing how scrupulously he gives Sogenes the exact measure of fit praise, he is in effect showing that he was not likely to have done less for Neoptolemos. For the myth just narrated, while it by no means ignored the element of error, even failure, in that hero's career, did bring it to a handsome conclusion. The debate which follows is admittedly difficult to epinician outsiders like ourselves, Pindaric *trobar clus*, and perhaps some of the plainer persons of Aigina were not entirely sure what the great man was going on about, though of course it was all very fine and anyway you could always concentrate on the dancing. But Pindar's true audience, the cognoscenti, would have seen what he was up to and delighted in his wit.

The passage is tidily plotted and consists of two pairs of opposing assertions. As often in Pindar, there is a firm logical structure so overlaid with detail and ornamentation that without digging down one may not mark it. Having just claimed that he has warded off censure, he now swings to the opposite pole and declares that he has not been guilty of overpraise:

No Akhaian from his Ionian seaboard
present today will blame me. I take my stand

on friendship's ground [*proxenia*]. Among our citizens
  too
my gaze is clear, untroubled. I have overstepped no
  mark,
thrust all violence from my path.

In plain prose, "no one will criticize me for going too far."
(Does the "violence" he has thrust from his path refer
obliquely to his treatment of Neoptolemos in the paian?) By
a common Greek idiom, "no one" is expressed by saying "no
one from far away and no one near at hand," and this lets
him introduce both the figure of the Akhaian, someone from
distant Epiros, one imagines, the kingdom of Neoptolemos
where any slur on his good name would be most keenly resented, and also the picture of himself on his usual cordial
terms with the citizens of Aigina. Having protested his innocence on this score, Pindar again clears himself of the con-
trary charge, drawing an image from his own art:

Let future time befriend me.
No one who understands will say I come
breaking the measure, jangling a tuneless discord.

He has not, that is, come to Aigina with a poem that tastelessly berated the victor. Nor, over once more to the opposite
pole, has he garishly belauded him. For turning now to the
victor himself, the name of whose family, the Euxenidai or
Hospitables, evokes the theme of guest-friendship, he begins:

Scion of the Eúxenid clan, my Sógenes!

and vehemently affirms that he has not overstepped the
mark, using terms from the event in which Sogenes obtained
his victory, the pentathlon. Any Aiginetan child could no
doubt have explained just what Pindar is saying here, but

sporting metaphors are seldom clear outside their place of origin ("snicking one through the slips," meaningless in America, is readily understandable in cricketing England) and scholars are still disputing exactly what the lines imply.

The debate is over and the poet, as though exhausted by his efforts, cries "Let me be!" With fine rhetorical skill he has maintained his innocence on two counts. To those who came to the performance convinced that he had previously misrepresented, underpraised, their hero Neoptolemos, he says with great sincerity that he has taken care not to do with Sogenes what Homer did with Odysseus: he has not . . . overpraised him. With equal sincerity he assures all and sundry that he has scrupulously avoided doing what no epinician poet who hoped to stay in business was ever likely to do, fail to praise his client warmly enough. His case rests, but he cannot forbear from adding one final flourish: "Let me be! If, for the victor's sake, I was carried away and uttered too loud a cry, I am ready to take it back."*

It is no argument against this interpretation, which assumes some truth in the story of Aiginetan indignation over the poet's treatment of Neoptolemos in a previous poem, that the debate is conducted in the familiar terms of epinician rhetoric—and hence should not be understood in some special, unusual sense. Of course it is so conducted, that is the point: what is normally a fiction is here unexpectedly applied to a real situation. In a context like this, "no one will blame me if" is a common encomiastic trope, as Bundy shows (II.40). It is bold and amusing to use this trope before an audience that has come prepared to blame you in earnest. An orator

*The verb I translate "take back" (*katathemen*) is usually understood as meaning "pay down my debt" or the like. My rendering follows Sandys, "I am not too rude to retract it," and Wilamowitz in a paper of 1908 on this ode, "will ich gern zurücknehmen."

emerging from a spell in a Trappist monastery would raise a laugh if he began, "Unaccustomed as I am to public speaking."

If I am right in finding wit in this passage, the wit lies in the way Pindar, as though walking a tightrope, suggests the extreme difficulty of the middle path he must take between two faulty extremes, one of which is purely imaginary, while the other, though I believe it has some substance, has been considerably exaggerated for the poem's rhetorical purposes. (If his earlier account of Neoptolemos' death had really outraged public opinion in the island, he would hardly have been invited back again.) Yet this witty play serves serious ends, for between the extremes of excessive and defective praise lies the measure of true praise, poetry's power to bear true witness, the deepest subject of this poem and the basis of the whole epinician art. Hence, the faulty extremes having been rejected, Pindar is free at last to address the victor in the proper terms. No more smiling now, for one of the richest passages of praise poetry in the odes is beginning:

> Weaving garlands for him is easy.
> > Let the lyre strike up. Look,
> to ivory and gold the Muse is binding
> delicate curl of the foam flower won from the sea.

This garland or crown is not an artifact which archaeologists might discover, as Wilamowitz supposed, but a purely poetic emblem embodying that combination of the ephemeral and permanent which is the epinician poet's final achievement. Or rather, as Pindar in his piety sees it, the Muse's achievement. Any singer can weave perishable garlands for a victor; the truly difficult task is to create, as the Muse does, a garland of such permanence—praise poetry of such accuracy and beauty—that men will preserve it forever. Note that for his

image of the ephemeral Pindar takes the most evanescent
thing imaginable, the flower-shaped pattern momentarily
formed by the ceaseless play of the waves, winning this
"flower," to be joined to incorruptible ivory and gold, from
what earlier had been the destructive element. (The flower is
not coral, as the scholiast's mistaken note has led too many
commentators and translators to understand it. A hard du-
rable substance is quite out of place here.)

A hush falls as the fourth and final movement of the ode
begins in hymnic form with a prayer to Zeus ("remembering
Zeus for Nemea's sake"). It is Zeus himself, father of the
Muses whose mother is Memory, who is to preside over this
great song of praise. ("The perfet witnes of all judging
Jove"—once again and even more strongly *Lycidas* comes to
mind.) The hymn is bidden to resound (*doneō*) quietly—or
perhaps vibrate, tremble, murmur, a delicately evocative
word Pindar had used of music in the tenth Pythian: "For it
is fitting that on this holy ground our voices proclaim the king
of the gods." It appears that the ode is being performed in
the holiest place in Aigina, the precinct of Aiakos or Aiakeion,
the square enclosure walled with white stone in the most
prominent part of the city, with an altar to the founding hero
set amid age-old olive trees. For the poet goes on: "They say
that Zeus planted Aiakos in the womb of Aigina—Aiakos, my
famous country's captain and, O Herakles, to be your kindly
friend (xeinos) and brother!" *My* country, Theban Pindar
makes bold to say (the manuscript reading, changed by too
many editors to "his"), so completely does he now feel himself to be identified with the island. (It may be easier though
it is not I think necessary to take this as an instance of the
choral "I.") To invoke Herakles is appropriate enough in any
epinician ode but there is a special point here, for the poet

tells us in one of his rare but precious townscapes that Sogenes' house stood between two shrines of the great hero:

> Within your care Sógenes will prosper
> (O You who brought the Giants down),
> tender in bounden duty to his father,
> keeping his ancestral house that stands
> in the rich and hallowed street between Your shrines,
> like the yoke-pole of a four-horse chariot.

The picture here conjured up, of a patriarchal almost hieratic way of life, is no doubt sufficiently unlike the bustling maritime center that was historical Aigina. Pindar's is an art of idealization, which is neither falsification nor flattery but a stripping away of the trivial and contingent to reach down to what he saw as the essential. Driven by a similar impulse, Piero della Francesca took Montefeltro's warty, self-satisfied face and broken nose and made a sacred icon of him. Pindar took Hieron of Syracuse and from his poor human clay fashioned a changeless work of art, a *daidalma*.* The young hero of the present occasion is no less strangely transformed. As we are made to see him, dwelling in his *via sacra* between the two shrines of Herakles—like Neoptolemos lying for ever in the holy soil of Delphi—Sogenes too has become almost a sacred presence, a figure of cult.

This glancing recall of the culminating movement of the myth prepares the way for the final lines of the ode, a kind of coda. After a conventional prayer that the victor's happi-

---

*The literal and real force of the verb *daidalōsemen* at Olympian 1.105, dulled by the scholiast into *kosmēsein*, embellish, honor—similarly Slater, "embellish, metaphorically, glorify." What scholarly principle requires that in poetry the most reductive meaning of a word is always the correct one? Only Curtis Bennett, so far as I am aware, has caught the force of the verb here (*God as Form* [1976], 102).

ness may endure from youth to sleek old age (a beautiful
replay in a different key of the initial movement from the birth
goddess to the death wave) and an equally conventional hope
for even greater victories to come, Pindar returns once more
to the accusation he had earlier made such fine sport of. No
argumentation now but smiling ease and a flick of contempt
for those who had entertained so improbable a story:

> Never will my heart say
> I mauled Neoptólemos with untoward words.
> But turning the same ground over and over
> 's a shiftless trick, like the tattler's tale
>   to children, *Children, Corinth belongs to God.*

A proverb used of those who keep repeating the same thing,
we are told, here no doubt serving too as a humorous example
of praise that tastelessly oversteps the measure. With these
trite words, half thrown away, one imagines, the music at last
falls silent as the dancers complete their final movements. The
performance is over.

Nemean 11: A Client Who Did Not Fit the Convention

The critical fashion today is to find Pindar everywhere
conforming closely to the rules of epinician grammar, and
odes once thought eccentric are now declared to be straightforward encomia. The poet, on this reading, was highly predictable. The victor handed in his specifications and paid his
fee and in due course one more regular epinician article rolled
off the Theban production line. Nemean 11, however, is allowed some curious features, at least by the better critics. It
is a poem, one writes, "in which Pindar places unusual emphasis on psychological motivation." This is not the only odd
thing about it, but certainly we are prompted to inquire, as

nowhere else in the odes, what sort of man the poet's client was (we cannot properly speak of a victor here) and what situation lies behind the poem. This is of course still public poetry and we are by no means to extract from it material for a short story in the manner of Henry James. A public poem composed in the fifth century B.C., Nemean 11 praises one Aristagoras of Tenedos. Having said this, as we must, we may go on to observe that the task of devising appropriate encomiastic terms for this man was unusually difficult. Where else do we find Pindar praising someone less for what he did than for what he might have done? It may even appear that Aristagoras is praised for what he did *not* do, for what in his wisdom he abstained from doing.

This ode is neither Nemean nor strictly epinician, since the victories it commemorates were won not in the great games but in local contests. Its occasion in fact is not primarily athletic at all. It celebrates Aristagoras' installation as president of the council at Tenedos, a small island off Asia Minor in the eastern Aegean, and the first two stanzas take the form of a prayer for the successful tenure of his one-year term of office. With the third stanza or epode, Aristagoras and his father are named and praised, the father for having such a son, the son for his fine physique and innate *atremia*, courage or fearlessness, as the word is usually understood. Pindar then declares:

> Yet even if a man is fortunate and comely beyond his
> fellows
> and winning first place in the games has proved his
> strength,
> let him remember that the limbs he clothes are mortal
> and that in the end he will put on a garland of earth.

This almost medieval reminder of our final estate seems out

of place in a Greek poem of the classical period ("Le squelette était invisible / Au temps heureux de l'Art païen"), but the scholiast's paraphrase shows that what we have here is a version of the ne plus ultra topic which is addressed to so many of Pindar's victors: "[Even if he is fortunate] let a man be aware that he is mortal and not seek for a greater happiness." The thrust, we have found, is normally not so much *Go no further!* as *Look how far you have come!* Normally, though, does not mean invariably, and we should allow for the possibility that these weighty and indeed somber lines with their reminder not simply of mortal limit but of mortality may not here have the sense we have learned to expect. A genre governed by strict conventions gives the poet a resource we deny him if we fail to see that he may sometimes use a familiar element in an unfamiliar way. A convention can be as valuable to the poet when, playing against expectation, he departs from it as when he observes it.

A limitary precept commonly occurs after the praise of high achievement and is most often placed, as William Mullen has taught us to see, in the epode, as it is here. But we cannot help wondering if Aristagoras' achievement really calls for so emphatic a statement, expressed in a way not found elsewhere in the odes. True, we have been told of some victories, but told briefly, almost cursorily; the stress has gone on his appointment as president of the council at Tenedos, no doubt a coveted post in the community but hardly such (we would suppose) as to transport the holder to the far reaches of felicity. We find that the poet does go on to speak at more length about his client's successes in the games. There were a great many of them, and briefly we hear the noble language of epinician triumph:

It is right he should win good report from the lips of
   his neighbors.
We must adorn this man with the douce-toned songs of
   praise.
For sixteen times the region's athletes have yielded
in the wrestler's bout and the proud pankration
victory's bright circlet
            to Aristágoras and his famous land.

Local victories, though, did not carry a great deal of prestige
and in a normal ode they are thrown in as something of a
makeweight. Given the number Aristagoras had won, it
would of course have been well within Pindar's powers to
make them sound very glorious indeed: *provided* he made no
mention of the great, far more glorious games. To our surprise, however, we hear him declare resoundingly that if Aristagoras had competed in the Pythian or Olympian games he
would have come home in triumph. A remarkable reason is
given for his not competing:

Too diffident the hopes of his parents held him back
   from trying his strength at Delphi or the games at
   Olympia.
Had he gone, by my oath I affirm he could have
   returned
garlanded.

This glimpse into a world which has room for faltering re-
solve, even for failure or something very like it, is unique in
Pindar and sets us asking questions we would not dream of
raising elsewhere. Aristagoras had presumably sanctioned the
reference to his father's diffidence. ("His parents," the Greek
says, but it seems unlikely that his mother can have had much

say in the matter.) Was papa aware of this interesting feature
of the commission and, if not, how did he react when the ode
was publicly performed? Had Aristagoras dutifully accepted
the paternal veto (he sighed as an athlete but obeyed as a
son), or had he strongly resented it and taken advantage of
the present occasion to get his own back? Diverting as it may
be, this line of inquiry can plainly not be pursued without
losing sight of our ode altogether. We still do need to ask,
though, why Pindar introduced the hazardous allusion to the
Pythian and Olympian games. The simplest answer is that he
was required to do so by Aristagoras, but we have to assume
that the poet knew how to handle his clients and admitted
into an ode only those elements which he judged would con-
tribute to its success. Unless Nemean 11 is to be written off
as a botched job, we must suppose that the pattern of praise
he had devised for his patron demanded this reference to the
final challenge which he did not face. To attribute this for-
bearance (should we call it?) to Aristagoras himself would
have been too damaging, so his father has to take the re-
sponsibility. This admittedly shows the old man in an unfa-
vorable light, but the poet's primary duty was to his patron.

Pindar now goes on to contrast two kinds of person.
There is the boaster who does not have it in him to make
good his empty claims, and there is the man who unduly
underrates his powers: "His timid heart drags him back, de-
priving him of the honors properly his." It is common in the
odes to find a virtue praised by setting it against an opposing
defect. In Nemean 3, for example, the man of inherited valor
is contrasted with the man who has merely been taught and
veers now here now there, trying his hand at a thousand
projects but never completing any of them. There, it is quite
clear that the victor is an example of the first kind of person;

it is much less clear in the present poem to which class Aristagoras belongs. Plainly he is not the boaster, but can he be the man held back by his timid heart? We are left wondering where, between these two extremes, to place him.

As the third and final triad opens, the poet tries another tack, still apparently defining the terms in which Aristagoras can be fittingly praised. Like other shorter odes Nemean 11 has no myth, the place where we look for the foundational event which made the victor what he was. Instead we have a few lines which might have furnished the material for a myth, a brief account of how Aristagoras' ancestors sailed from mainland Greece to colonize Tenedos. It is easy to tell, Pindar affirms, that his blood derives from that heroic stock. He goes on, once again leaving us uncertain how to take his words:

> The ancient virtues
> send up their strength for the generations of men
> in alternation. Not always do the dark ploughlands
>   grant their harvest
> nor as the years come round will trees bear fruit and
>   scented blossom
> always, in equal yield.
>   So fate steers the course of human kind.

That a principle of alternation governs human affairs is a familiar thought in the odes, though the figure through which it is here expressed is found only once elsewhere, in Nemean 6. There it is said of the young victor fresh from his triumph that "he bears witness to the genius of his breed, that it resembles the fruitful fields which now grant men their yearly provender, now lie at rest regaining strength." The boy's grandfather, it appeared, was a great athlete whereas his father had not distinguished himself; having lain fallow for a generation, the family is now fruiting richly again. This, we suppose, must be the official, uppermost meaning here too, and yet once more we are left doubtful. Can this modestly successful man who did *not* cross the sea and risk the supreme throw at one of the great festivals be said—except at the level of hollow flattery—to recall the ancestral heroes who sailed from Sparta and Thebes to found Tenedos? Their strength may still be in him but it is, relatively, lying fallow.

Our doubts about the poet's direction increase in the final stanza, though the writing is powerful and he seems to know exactly where he is going. He begins by clinching the preceding lines with a brief statement of the uncertainty principle: "No clear sign from Zeus guides men on their way." Again a familiar saying. In Olympian 12, using similar language ("No man has won from the gods a clear token of things to come"), he had spoken of the way our hopes are tossed up and down as we voyage across a treacherous sea. Uncertainty, for Greek thought, the changeable weather of mortal existence, was not depressing or frightening, as it was to be for Christians, for if joy does not last, neither does sorrow. As Olympian 12 expresses it:

> Much comes upon us beyond expectation,
> joy turns widdershins.
>
>   He who has faced the bitter surge may soon
> win a deep gladness for the pain he had.

In Nemean 11 too Pindar is thinking of the sea, that great visible image of vicissitude never far from Greek eyes or Greek minds, but the tone is darker: "And yet we embark on great endeavours, desiring many things. For our limbs are bound by cruel hope; far from foreknowledge the streams on which we sail." "Hope," as the Greek word (*elpis*) is conven-

tionally translated, the faculty by which we seek to get a hold
on a future beyond our control, did not offer the Greek much
comfort. Elpis may mean, neutrally, expectation, or, as it does
here, something like delusion and as such it can be coupled
with *erōs*, not simply "love" but the passion of desire or longing, frequently for something beyond our reach or best not
reached for. Together these two drives, daemonic in their
power over us, lead to the ruinous sometimes glorious actions
on which Greek tragic thought so often dwells. Sophocles
couples them when he says that hope "cheats us with its
madcap longings" (*Antigone*, 617). So in a famous sentence
does Thucydides: "Hope and Desire are everywhere at work,
Desire leading, Hope following, Desire devising the scheme
while Hope suggests that luck is sure to point the way. These
two powers are the most harmful, for being invisible they
count for more than the dangers men can see" (*The Peloponnesian War*, 3.45). Pindar too, in the last line of the poem, having
spoken of the cruelty of hope, is led to exclaim:

> Too cruel the madness that yearns for what lies beyond
> reach.

Against these passions he can offer nothing except the traditional counsel: "We must seek for measure in our win-
nings." Measure, a fragile check on the all but ungovernable
démesure which possesses us.

We read badly if we do not find ourselves perplexed at
this point, wondering what Pindar is doing in this unfamiliar
territory and, still more, how all this applies to Aristagoras.
Magistrate in his remote community, victor in a number of
regional games, what ruinous passion for the unattainable
touched the life of this man? The difficulty is no less if we ask
rather, as we should, what terms of praise are these that Pindar has devised for him. Is he simply telling him that, al-

though he has not won any of life's supreme prizes, he should
be satisfied with what he has got and not ask for more? Surely
the man expected something better than this dusty piece of
advice when he put down his drachmas. Nothing in the ode
as we have been reading it or as it is usually read satisfactorily
explains what Pindar is doing, and the only course is to retrace our steps and go back to the beginning, looking for what
we have missed.

The ode starts with a prayer to Hestia, "whose portion is
the hall of cities, sister of Zeus most high and of Hera throned
beside him." In literal translation this sounds far from promising, but Pindar's preludes take close attention and are almost always saying something that should direct our sense of
everything that follows. For whatever reason, Nemean 11 begins with Hestia, Hearth, and her cult at Tenedos. Of this
cult Farnell remarks that it throws light "on a certain primitive
phase of religious thought," providing a glimpse of "a world
of religious feeling difficult for us to understand" (*The Cults
of the Greek States*, V.345, 364). Farnell was writing around the
turn of the century, in the final afterglow of the Enlighten-
ment, and the difficulty he experienced in entering this
"primitive" world has perhaps diminished since his day, if
only because so many of the obstructive certainties he felt
assured of have collapsed. Living at a time of cultural disarray,
we are better able to respond sympathetically to other systems
of belief and conduct. To enter into the thought of this ode
we must at all events try to do so.

The word *hestia* simply means "hearth," and Hestia is not
so much the goddess as the embodied sanctity of the hearth,
the household hearth and more particularly the communal
hearth where, as the scholiast tells us, "what is called the
sacred fire" was kept burning. We must make of this what

we can. Hestia is asked to welcome to her chamber Aristagoras and the other members of the council "who honor you
and keep Tenedos upright. It is you they worship first of the
gods, with libations often and often with savor of sacrifice.
At their bidding the lyre resounds, and song. And the rite of
Zeus Xenios, Lord of Guest and Host, is observed at your
table whose bounty does not fail. May Aristagoras come in
glory to the end of his twelve-month term with heart un-
scathed." Just as in a regular epinician, these lines direct our
attention to the figure for whom the ode is being performed.
Not that Hestia and her cult are background or foil, to be set
aside once we get to Aristagoras; they are part and parcel of
him, they enter into his life-substance and explain him. For
the president of the council was not simply a magistrate; his
office must have been as much priestly as administrative. And
Tenedos (the lines tell us), the homeland that made him what
he was and where he belonged in a sense of belonging closer
than any we know—Tenedos was a place where the cult of
Hestia was zealously preserved and taken very seriously. Her
cult was practiced elsewhere in Greece, of course (in up-to-
date Athens, for example), but perhaps in a remote, old-fashioned place like Tenedos, practiced with a special purity. As
we meditate these lines and listen to their slow grave music,
the spirit of the place—archaic, traditional, patriarchal—begins to come alive for us.

With the final section of the first triad Pindar turns directly to Aristagoras and his father. He praises Aristagoras,
as we saw, for his "wonderful body," his fine physique, and
for his inherited or innate atremia. The lexicon takes the word
to mean a "keeping still," with the special sense here of "in-
trepidity" (a translation of the scholiast's gloss). Slater suggests "steadfastness" as an alternative. If that is all the word
means, it is simply a routine term of praise and claims no

special attention. A different rendering was long ago proposed by Otto Schroeder in his edition of the odes, but it
seems to have received little attention: *innata animi tranquillitas.* This is decidedly more interesting and it is supported by
the meaning of the verb *atremizein* in Herodotos. Herodotos
uses it to describe the aggressive, expansionist thrust which
he saw in Persian policy and thought inherent in great political power. He says of the Persian power in his *Histories* that
"it did not remain quiet or inactive" (*ouk atremizousan*, 1.185),
and a few chapters later, of Cyrus the founder of the empire,
that he did not "remain inactive" (*ouk atremizonta*) but was
always aiming at fresh conquests (1.190). The word occurs
again in a debate preceding the second Persian invasion of
Greece as Xerxes tells his assembled nobles: "I learn from our
elders that since we took over supreme power from the Medes
we have never been inactive" (*oudama kō ētremisamen*, 7.8). A
wise counselor seeks to dissuade Xerxes from the proposed
campaign but then, influenced by a dream which appears
both to the king and to himself, recants. He opposed the
expedition, he explains, "because I know that to long for
many things is an evil . . . and I thought that if you remained
quietly at peace [*atremizonta*] everyone would call you a fortunate man. But since a daemonic power thrusts us forward . . . I have changed my mind and withdraw my former
counsel" (7.18).

Earlier on Herodotos said the same thing about the
growth of Spartan power, using a more familiar word: "Since
their soil was good and their male population large, they shot
up quickly and flourished. No longer, then, content to live
quietly" (*hēsukhiēn agein*), they set about assaulting their next-
door neighbors (1.66). This restless, aggressive drive which
Herodotos more or less dispassionately observed as something which comes on men when they reach a certain level

of power and prosperity, Thucydides saw in darker colors as
a predominant trait of the Athenian empire. The Athenians,
he reports the Corinthians as saying, "can neither live quietly
themselves [*ekhein hēsukhian*] nor let anyone else do so" (1.70).
Not content with what they have, they are always reaching out
for more, for greater things (*tou pleonos ōregonto, meizonōn ōregonto*), he says of them several times. Whether or not he saw
this drive in the half-poetic, tragic terms which Cornford
attributed to him, for the poets at any rate the aggressive
reach for more pointed beyond politics to something written
deeply into human nature, that soaring discontent with man's
limited condition which is at once the mark of our greatness
and the high road to ruin. At its fullest stretch, it is the desire
for transcendence or, to say it in Greek, the desire to become
god.

And this is what seems to be at issue in the lines at the
end of Nemean 11, un-Pindaric as such aspirations may appear. For after praising Aristagoras for his atremia—his animi
tranquillitas or *hēsukhia*, let us now take the word to mean—
the poet comes out with the powerful lines we have listened
to already:

Yet even if a man is fortunate and comely beyond his
    fellows. . . .

I previously quoted the scholiast's paraphrase. In fact, he provides a second: "[Let a man be aware that he is mortal.] Let
him not, like a god, reach out for greater things" (*mē hōs theos
tōn meizonōn oregesthō*). Perhaps we can now understand why
these lines sound so somber. It is because for once they really
are what they seem to be, a warning against the supreme sin
of attempting to transcend the human condition. Not of
course that Pindar is warning Aristagoras; that would be quite
out of place in an encomiastic ode. He is praising—in his

customary way praising a virtue by setting it against the opposing vice. On the one hand, serene acceptance of our condition; on the other, the impious longing to reach beyond it.
Some critics have found this passage out of keeping with the
opening of the poem. Wrongly, I think; what is now said of
Aristagoras is quite in harmony with what we were told about
his homeland. Whatever may be happening in other parts of
Greece (it would be helpful to know the date of this poem;
more on this a little later), at Tenedos the traditional virtues
are practiced and held in honor, above all by that wise and
fortunate man Aristagoras.

The next triad shows these virtues in action. Gifted with
fine athletic powers, Aristagoras was nonetheless content
with his numerous but relatively modest successes in the local
games. The question of why Pindar risked mentioning the
great games in which his client did not compete now has its
answer: Delphi and Olympia, elsewhere in the odes representing the highest human reach, here represent, almost,
overreach. Almost, because even in this unusual poem Pindar
cannot bring himself to condemn what he had spent his life
praising, so he tells us not that Aristagoras himself declined
to face the supreme challenge but that he was prevented from
doing so, held back by his father's diffidence. An uncomfortable item in an encomiastic ode, but the pattern of praise
required it. We can also see why Pindar goes on as he does,
with the contrast between the boaster who overrates his powers and the timorous man who underrates them. Between
braggart Too Much and craven Too Little, Aristagoras steers
his wise middle way. Not that the power of overreach is lacking in him; his is no eunuch virtue. The old strengths are still
there but they serve not for excess but for that noble virtue
which Greece called *sōphrosunē,* "man's pride," Camus

called it, "which is fidelity to his limits, lucid love of his condition."

What makes Nemean 11 difficult is not simply that it says unfamiliar things but that it does so by means of familiar topics and motifs which are turned about and made to point in unexpected directions. Thus in the powerful final stanza it is said that "we embark on great endeavors." Both figure and diction recall the praise of the victor in Nemean 3 who "went to the top of man's endeavor" ("embarked on," one might also translate). There, in the normal fashion, the supreme achievement was followed by a statement of limit: "Hard it is / to pass further on trackless water beyond the pillars" set up by Herakles as marking the boundary of permitted navigation. This was a way of signaling that he had done all that a man can do; there was no sense of any temptation to pass beyond this point, for the poet at once went on to tell how the greatest of heroes, having set up his pillars, "reached the bounds that sent him home." As I argued in my reading of that ode, the boundaries which circumscribe the Pindaric universe are not felt as restrictions; they mark out the arena in which great action can take place. Here, on the other hand, it is said that we embark on our ambitious ventures "desiring many things." (To long for many things is an evil, the wise Persian told Xerxes.) Recognizing no limit, we are driven forward into these unknown waters by cruel delusion which holds us fast, impelled—the strongest statement is kept for the last line—by the madness which makes us long for what lies beyond reach.

There is no difficulty in understanding why Pindar should decide to praise Aristagoras' virtues by setting them against the opposing offense. But what makes him condemn this offense so passionately? There is an intensity in the final line, a note of shocked revulsion, almost a cry of pain, which seems to go beyond anything the poem requires.* However we come at it, Nemean 11 leaves us with a sense of something still to be explained. Turn to a more famous, more lucid poem, the third Pythian, which also speaks powerfully of limit and the violation of limit. Written for Hieron of Syracuse, who was gravely, perhaps mortally, ill, the poem begins with a wish that he might recover. Innocent though it may appear, this wish is shown by a couple of related stories—about the great healer Asklepios and his mother Koronis—to be not only impossible but impious, a refusal of the terms on which man lives. Koronis, one of the shiftless breed of those who "pursue wind-borne phantoms with hopes not to be fulfilled," was with child by Apollo, but not content with her present good she refused to wait till the god found her a human husband. She wanted something more and secretly took a lover. Retribution came swiftly upon her. Asklepios was guilty of a like offense; for not content with his miraculous powers of healing he brought back to life a man already claimed by death, and he too was punished. It is at this point that Pindar breaks out with the famous lines which provided Valéry with the epigraph for the "Le cimitière marin":

χρὴ τὰ ἐοικότα πὰρ
   δαιμόνων μαστευέμεν θναταῖς φρασίν
γνόντα τὸ πὰρ ποδός, οἵας εἰμὲν αἴσας.
μή, φίλα ψυχά, βίον ἀθάνατον
σπεῦδε, τὰν δ᾽ ἔμπρακτον ἄντλει μαχανάν.

[We must ask from the gods things fitting our mortal

---

*Wilamowitz sensed the intensity of these words, understanding them as the expression of Pindar's own unattainable longings for a youth called Theoxenos, supposedly Aristagoras' brother, to whom he addressed a poem (*Pindaros*, 433). So personal an interpretation now strikes us as misguided; we may still learn from Wilamowitz' response to the Greek.

minds, knowing what lies to hand and what is granted
us. Do not, dear heart, strive for immortal life; use to the
full the means in your power.]

Since the passage has resisted all English translators, it is
worth quoting the conclusion of Romagnoli's Italian version
which conveys more of what is said there and the way it is
said:

> Non chiedere, o cuore diletto, la vita perenne,
> ma esercita l'opra concessa.

Speaking from the heart of Greek culture at its greatest, Pindar's words are grave, certainly, but they are marked by a
deep assurance, an utter calm. The sin of Koronis and Asklepios was the worst man can commit, but its dimensions had
long been plotted, its place on the moral map was well established, and the saving doctrine stood ready to meet it, enun-
ciated in these nobly sententious lines and embodied in a
contrasting pair of myths, the myth about Koronis and Asklepios and one concerning Peleus and Kadmos. Together
they teach that serene acceptance of the necessary in which
our well-being lies.

Nemean 11 offers something very different. The right
course is not traced nearly so luminously, for although Aristagoras' quiet virtues are genuine enough they cannot but
appear in a somewhat ambiguous light. And the contrasting
offense, the madness that yearns for what lies beyond reach,
is not really presented—embodied—in the poem at all but
seems rather to force its way into it, an alien visitant that
must be expelled at all costs. If this is so, it can only mean
that whatever it is that has so far puzzled us in Nemean 11
is not to be found in the poem itself but must be sought
outside it.

If it were written at a time when Athenian imperial am-
bitions were transforming the Greek world and threatening
the values which Pindar held dear, say around the middle of
the century, this would do a good deal to explain why he
praised Aristagoras as he did, contrasting his noble restraint
with the hateful overreach then all too much in evidence in
the political sphere. The poem has in fact until recently been
assigned a date of this sort (446 has been a popular year), but
the grounds for doing so now seem unpersuasive and are
anyway quite unlike my own. The interpretation I have proposed does not require us to read the poem against a particular political situation. Warnings about the dangers of
transgressive ambition had long been heard in Greek culture,
wise acceptance of human limit praised well before Athens
acquired an empire. Faced with the task of finding the right
encomiastic terms for his unusual client, Pindar could at any
period of his life and at any time during the century have
drawn on these old themes and turned them to his purpose.
All we can say is that contemporary circumstance would have
given them a sharper edge. To claim more would be unwise.

VI PYTHIAN 8:
THE FALL OF
THE LEAF

PINDAR SOMETIMES BEGINS AN ODE BY INVOKING WHAT WE
would call an abstraction or hypostatized essence or state,
Youthful Prime in Nemean 8, Divine One in Isthmian 5, Fortune in Olympian 12. Pythian 8, for an Aiginetan called Aristomenes, victor in the wrestling, begins with an invocation
to Hesukhia, Tranquillity or Calm, "who makes cities great,
the daughter of Justice." Not a promising start, to our minds,
conjuring up the disembodied females cultivated by neoclassical poets ("Hail, Contemplation, heav'nly Maid!"). If such
personifications are felt to be empty it is because they represent, long after the mind has learned to conceptualize, a
vain attempt to recover an earlier mode of thinking, essen-
tially the archaic mode. This was the way Pindar thought, one
still vital though its day was soon to pass. The canonical
model for this kind of thinking he found in Hesiod. In the
Theogony Hesiod relates how Zeus, having defeated the Titans
and then, a still more formidable foe, Typhon, set about establishing a stable, prosperous world. Hesiod expresses this
by saying that he married a series of divine ladies, among
them Themis (Order) who bore him Eunomia (Good Law),
Dika (Justice) and Eirene (Peace), and the three Fates. He also
married Eurunome (Wide Sway) who bore the three Graces,
and Memory, mother of the Muses (*Theogony,* 901–917). These
divinized beings are abstractions only in the sense of being
the concretion of a great many particulars. The Graces *are* the

energy that sends up the fruits of the earth for man and beast, they are whatever makes life joyful and "gracious," and for Pindar certainly they are limbs moving in the ordered measure of dance, voices lifted in the song that celebrates victory. To say that Zeus begot the Graces is to say that he brought into existence a world in which these good things can occur. Archaic thought is fully capable of generalization and its own kind of abstraction from experience, as all thinking must be, but it is grounded in and never moves far away from the world of living particulars, as conceptual thought so readily does.

Pindar's Hesukhia, daughter of Justice, belongs recognizably to this Hesiodic company, and whatever her role in the poem—a question we must expect the poem itself to answer—it is likely that she represents the same civilizing forces. A political virtue, then, in the Greek sense, and in Pindar's day something of a conservative catchword, denoting tranquillity and order within a city and the absence of party strife. Pindar's hosts, members of Aigina's ruling oligarchy, would have taken the invocation of Hesukhia as the poet's way of praising their community.

The term may in addition have a political sense extending beyond the confines of the city. In discussing the kindred term atremia in Nemean 11, we noted Thucydides' description of the Athenians as a people who could not live quietly (ekhein hesukhian) themselves or let anyone else do so. Thucydides reports Alcibiades speaking in the same vein when he tells the Athenians that you do not maintain an empire by keeping quiet (hesukhiazein, The Peloponnesian War, 6.18). Less overtly political but still with clear political overtones is the passage in the Birds of Aristophanes where it is said of the aerial city founded by the two Athenian dropouts, tired of their contentious city, that here is everything the heart can desire: Wis-

dom, the Graces, and "the bright face of kindhearted Calm"
(Hesukhia, 1318–1322).

It would seem, then, that Hesukhia represents a quietist,
"escapist" state of mind, and there were those in Athens who
saw her in that way. The opening of Pythian 8 shows that for
Pindar Hesukhia is a positive, active virtue:

> Calm of the tranquil kindly heart
>   daughter of Justice
> with you the city prospers and grows tall.
> In debate and battle
>   you hold the master keys.
> Receive this honored Pythian crown that Aristómenes
>   brings you.
> Gently you act and bear
>   doing as you would be done by
> both at the perfect season.
>
> But the man whose heart is rammed
> with rancorous hate, should he
> fall foul of you, harshly
> you front the attack and pitch
> Pride in the deep.

Pindar is not saying simply that Hesukhia can defend herself
when attacked. How forceful a principle she represents is
shown by the way he at once translates this seemingly abstract conflict between Calm and Pride (*hubris*) into dramatic
mythical terms:

>   Porphýrion
> the Giant King did not know your rule,
> he vexed you past all measure.
>   (What profits most is

the gift we take freely granted from a homestead.
But Too-Sure-of-Himself gets a tumble at your rough
   hands in time.)
Typhon that great worm did not escape you
for all his hundred heads. No, nor Porphýrion.
                   Thunder laid them low
and the arrows of Apollo. . . .

We are not told the crime for which they are punished, but
the homely gnomic insertion, applying to any act of robbery
or aggression, must have some bearing on it. Of Porphyrion's
offense there are different versions (according to one he tried
to rape Hera), but Pindar is clearly associating him with the
chaos dragon Typhon and about his offense there is no doubt.
It is the greatest, the primal offense, cosmic disorder assaulting heaven and trying to overturn cosmic order, for which,
as "the enemy of the gods," he received the portentous pun-
ishment described in Pythian 1. It seems likely that Typhon
and his fellow sinner are guilty of the same crime here, for it
is the gods, acting to enforce the principle embodied by Hesukhia, who bring them down. Only Apollo is mentioned—
piety required that he be praised in a poem celebrating a
Pythian victory—but Zeus too is involved, for the thunderbolt
is his weapon.

    Though daring, the ascription to Hesukhia of such
mighty powers is comprehensible if we have in mind her kinship with Hesiod's divine ladies. Pythian 8, however, is not
an ode to Hesukhia but a victory poem for an Aiginetan called
Aristomenes, and it is not yet clear what relevance Hesukhia
and her doings have to the occasion. Noting the wrestling
term used to describe her handling of Too-Sure-of-Himself,
we may be led to see the defeat which she and the gods inflict
on the two anarchs as an analogue of Aristomenes' defeat of

his opponents in the ring. But although Pindar pitches the
claims he makes for his victors very high, this is hardly the
sort of comparison he makes (if we except Pythian 1 where
he judged that Hieron had to be praised in the most grandiose
way possible). It would scarcely be decorous and to the poet
who wrote "Do not try to become Zeus" might well have
seemed impious. Some relevance this brief but powerful passage must however have, and perhaps we should understand
it as an example of Pindar's way of praising a virtue by setting
it against its opposite. On the one hand, there is the ugly
discordant world of the defeated agents of chaos, on the other,
as Apollo turns on his heel, the most exquisite turn in Pindar,
and ———. But we must have the poet's own way of putting
it:

> and the arrows of Apollo who of his good will
> received your son, Xenárkes, as he brought
> Delphi's crown of bay and a Dorian triumph song.

Two pictures. Here, the defeated sinners laid low by Apollo,
there the victorious Aristomenes welcomed by Apollo as he
comes from the serenely ordered world of the games. (With
this we hear the first note of a new theme, the Janus-like
relation between victory and defeat.) The contrast first stated
generally in terms of Hesukhia's two attributes, her gentle-
ness and her harshness, is now in Pindar's way translated
into these two contrasting pictures or actions, both revealing
her powers. If the connection between that defeat and this
victory still seems somewhat remote, we may compare a passage in Olympian 13 where the victor's athletic success is seen
to be grounded in the fact that his city honors Hesukhia's
Hesiodic kin, Eunomia, Dika, and Eirene, and opposes brash-
tongued Hubris.

Only one triad read so far, with four more to come, but

already we have the tentative sense that large issues may be involved. Securely enough assigned to the year 446, when Pindar was 72, Pythian 8 is the latest datable poem. We expect, in the late work of a great master, to see him reaching for some final statement, a summation of all that life has taught him. And, it seems almost to be a rule, this more comprehensive wisdom will be accompanied by an even greater command of his medium. Hence, if it should prove that the epinician form is here being stretched to say more than it had ever said before, this will in no way involve any neglect of the genre's conventions. They are likely to be treated with supreme ease and mastery, as they are here. The first triad has deftly taken care of the victor's name, the festival in which he won, the type of contest (Too-Sure-of-Himself's "tumble" tells us that Aristomenes was a wrestler), his father's name, name of the presiding god. Until the introduction of the poem's principal myth at the end, the second triad is entirely filled with these conventional elements—conventional, and yet each one expressive as hardly before. The poet handles these well-worn tools of his trade, the topics of his epinician art, as though they had been fashioned for this occasion only.

First, praise of the victor's homeland. Pindar employs a curious figure:

> She fell not far from the Graces,
> this island city where Justice lives,
> the valor of the sons of Aíakos
> holding her straitly.

Why is Aigina praised for having *fallen*? Plainly a metaphorical fall, but what is the metaphor? Commentators seem mostly to agree that we are to think of the fall of the dice, but this answers to nothing in the poem's imagery. Since it is "not far

from the Graces"—spirits of growth and fertility—that Aigina
fell, it is tempting to think that the metaphor is that of the
fall of the seed, as in Olympian 7 where the words of the gods
concerning Rhodes "fell in truth" and at once the island
"grew" from the sea bed. In Nemean 7, however, the seed is
said to be planted by Zeus in the womb of Aigina. Can Aigina
be both the seed and the womb that receives the seed? Logically, no, but Pindar's thinking about these ancestral heroines, at once a mass of earth and stone and the bride of deity
and mother of a line of heroes, is at the extreme limit of our
understanding and he might have seen nothing contradictory
about speaking of Aigina, the source of new, continuing life,
in one place as the seed-bearer and here, if I am right, as the
seed: it fell in fertile soil and fruited richly.

A fortunate fall, then, Aigina's, and an emphatic one:
"fell" is in Greek the first word of the new triad. Looking
ahead we find another fortunate fall in the opening line of
the final triad, the victor's. He too fell—on the prostrate bodies of his opponents. A little later he rises, flies indeed, and
there is one more fall, a darker or sadder one. We hear too of
God the Wrestler—a grand figure first discerned, I believe,
by Ruck and Matheson—who throws one man up, another
down. (Like the heaven-storming sinners, laid low by the
thunderbolt and by the arrows of Apollo.) There is a lot of
rising and falling in this poem, a good deal too about victory
and defeat, and inevitably our minds connect the two pairs.
Several falls, some fortunate, and in the main myth a victory
with misfortune at the heart of it. A pattern is starting to
emerge, though we do not yet know what it means.

Pindar continues his praise of the homeland with something he had held to all his life but never expressed so briefly
and with such authority, the simultaneous existence of origin,
arkha, and end, telos:

τελέαν δ' ἔχει
δόξαν ἀπ' ἀρχᾶς.

Aigina *perfectam habet gloriam ab initio*. Fifty years earlier, in
the poem we take to be his first, Pythian 10, he had said much
the same thing, very simply, and yet we must call typography
to our aid to convey what is said there:

our end & origin

(to) ripeness   grow

at the god thrust.

Origin and end are not stationed at opposing points on a line;
they coexist, the end already present in the origin. Nor is the
end a goal in the sense of something reached finally and once
and for all, a termination; it is reached again and again, with
Aristomenes' victories today and with tomorrow's victories,
if there are victories tomorrow. All this is said still more con-
cisely in Pythian 8's consummate statement. Here, instead of
treating origin and end as separate even though inseparable
entities, Pindar fuses them by making "end" an adjective
modifying the island's original, originating glory. At the origin (when Zeus planted his seed in the island's ancestral heroine), Aigina's glory was already final, *perfecta*.

Some more swift words of praise—for the island's old
heroes and the living heroes of the day—cut short by a familiar device, the break-off formula as we call it, but the imperious words and rhythm make our critical term look even
more ungainly than usual:

Time scants me to set up
for lyre and liquid voice so long a story
lest chafing surfeit come.

Yet another conventional element follows, the *khreos-* or debt-motif. One of the densest and most brilliant bits of writing in Pindar, it had best be translated as literally as possible: "But this thing which runs at my feet, your khreos, youngest of [Aigina's] glories/beauties, let it go forward, child, winged by my art." The uppermost sense of khreos is debt, the debt of song which the poet owes the victor. It is at the poet's feet in the sense that it is the immediate task at hand, as we would say; it runs because it is pressing, urgent. In poetry khreos can also mean "business, affair," so that there is a secondary sense, "this business of yours, your victory." It runs because victory, the glory of victory, is of all things the most transient and will run away unless the poet secures, stays, it with his song. Song arrests victory's transience and by making it winged—a figure Pindar uses several times—gives it a longer, even an immortal life. This is paradoxical, though; a flying object is gone even more quickly than one that merely runs. A paradox indeed, one the poet had been at grips with all his life, the relation between transience and permanence which is at the heart of the victory celebration, marriage of a momentary glitter and an enduring text. The relation touches our condition at the quick and poetry has always been engaged with it. The poet may bid himself or the beloved seize the speeding moment (Gather ye rosebuds), or he may bid it stay—"Verweile doch, du bist so schön!" A subtler tactic is to collaborate with transience, as Stevens does when he speaks of "a permanence composed of impermanence." Or as Marvell does, more powerfully, when he makes the lover tell his mistress that they can fight against time which passes so swiftly only by intensifying the speed of its passage:

> Thus, though we cannot make our Sun
> Stand still, yet we will make him run.

Pindar does much the same thing: he too intensifies tran-

sience to the point where it becomes a promise of permanence. This sort of verbal complexity, so common in the best
English poetry, is, I am aware, not supposed to occur in Greek
poetry—perhaps because those capable of recognizing it have
usually not known enough Greek to find it there while those
with the necessary Greek are often strangely innocent about
the devious ways of poetry.

The second triad ends as the poet, still addressing the
victor, tells him that his feats in the wrestling have earned
him the fame that the prophet Amphiaraos once ————. And
the myth begins, coming in on its relative pronoun, and fills
two-thirds of the next triad. It has often been noticed that
alone of Pindar's eleven Aiginetan odes Pythian 8 does not
draw its myth from the island's saga. If we are to seek a
reason for this, it may be that he needed some especially close
consonance between myth and theme. The sort of fit that
served well in a poem like Nemean 3, for example, will not
do; Achilles' exploits as boy hunter and as full-grown warrior
accounted quite sufficiently for the *virtù* of the Aiginetan victor in that poem, but other Aiakid doings would have served
equally well. Here, the poet may have needed a tale that
hewed more closely to his theme, and not finding it in the
island's legendary went to Thebes for it and chose the story
of the assault on the city by the successors of the famous
Seven, the Epigonoi. The myth is narrated by the prophet
Amphiaraos who took part and died in the first attack, an
oracular utterance delivered from his tomb, we may suppose.
Watching the successors fight, his son Alkman—like himself,
both warrior and prophet—assaulting the gates, he declares:

> Sire to son, innate
> the noble temper shines.

This is the myth's primary theme and it does nothing to sup-

port my contention that Pindar needed a story with some
special point or twist to it, for the force of heritage is something he often dwells on. ("The man of breed walks in his
father's footsteps," for example, in Pythian 10, or "There's a
weight of inherited glory in the race," from Nemean 3.) The
myth has however a second theme. The expedition of the
Seven against Thebes failed, that of the Epigonoi succeeded,
but success was flawed since their leader, Adrastos, saw his
son fall in the action. Prophetically Amphiaraos says:

> Alone of all that band
> he will gather the bones of his son, then by God's
>   grace
> lead home his force unscathed
> to the broad streets of Argos.

Victory with sorrow and loss for the victor—perhaps it is this
feature of the story that made Pindar choose his Theban myth:
its contribution to the poem's thematic pattern that is unfold-
ing before our eyes: rising/falling, victory/defeat, happy or
victorious falls (Aigina's, not far from the Graces; the victor's,
on the bodies of his opponents), and now this sorrowful victory.

The transition from the myth back to the victor takes an
unusual form. Instead of the gnomic reflection we might expect, no sooner has Amphiaraos fallen silent than the poet
declares: "And gladly I also garland Alkman and shower him
with song. For he is my neighbor and guardian of my goods.
He came to meet me as I was on my way to earth's famous
navel-stone and plied the prophetic skill that he had by inheritance." (The myth's first theme again.) What are we to
make of this encounter? It may well be that, as Aristomenes'
loyal friend, Pindar did indeed go to Delphi to watch him
compete there, and it is not impossible that on the way he

"met"—had a vision of—the prophet Alkman (an experience
that would have seemed less outré to Pindar's listeners than
it does to us) and learned from him how the contest would
turn out. What else can the content of Alkman's prophecy
have been? However this may be, it is likely that we should
think of this journey to Delphi as primarily a rhetorical or
symbolical one. In other words, Pindar is doing what we saw
him do in Nemean 7, presenting a development in the poem
he is composing, the transition back to the victor, as an action
undertaken by himself.

As the fourth triad opens, then, we are to imagine the
poet—the poem—at Delphi, preparing to recreate in art's du-
rable terms the brief flash of Aristomenes' victory. First there
must be a prayer to the presiding deity, Apollo, in whose
honor the Pythian festival was held. Piety required the prayer,
epinician convention looked for the victory list in this part of
an ode. The prayer accordingly introduces two elements in
the list. "There you granted him the greatest of joys," his
present Delphic victory, Pindar says, and recalls an earlier
success which the god gave Aristomenes in the local games
at Aigina; the triad will end with three further victories. This
is a high moment for the young man, and it is one of the
places in an ode where we easily go wrong by not heeding
the presence of a very Greek dialectical train of thought. A
high moment, and so calling for praise. High, hence perilous.
(It is God's way to bring down whatever is too tall, Herodotos
says.) Yet only great men face such perils. (Praise.) Nonetheless, peril is there and in the interests of his client the poet
must go carefully, so he asks the god to grant him the proper
proportion in his praise, neither too much nor too little:

> Lord, I pray this be your will:
> Let your eyes look down a measure
> on every step I take.

Measure must govern the whole celebration:

> Beside this troop that sweetly sounds
> triumph's song   Justice stands.

Justice, *Dika*, mother of Hesukhia who rules over the orderly
world of the games and, as we saw in the first triad, overrules
the presumption of those who reach too high. So, turning to
the victor's father, Pindar goes on: "I pray, Xenarkes, that
heaven's envy may not mar your family's good fortune." (God
will have no one think big except himself, Herodotos says.)
Aristomenes has been richly successful, but success is God's
good gift. We must sweat for it, of course—a few parenthetical
words dismiss the sort of fellow who thinks to win "with no
great labor." But these things are not in our hands, the poet
says piously, and proceeds to introduce the remarkable figure
of God the Wrestler, to show Aristomenes and the rest of us
how victory comes about: God tosses this man up and that
man down—a replay in a different key of the two contrasting
motions in the first triad, the heaven stormers brought down
by the god who graciously welcomes the victor fresh from his
triumph. The pattern in the weave is beginning to stand out.
Plainly it must represent vicissitude, the two-way movement
of things, a constant in Pindar's poetry, but we may wonder
why he is insisting on it so strongly here.

And the pattern stands out still more plainly as, after
only a light pause, the fifth and final triad begins with another
wrestler in action, Aristomenes himself this time, enacting by
his motions in the ring the metaphorical, thematic motions
the poet has devised to celebrate his victory:

> What a high grim fall it was!
> you came down on those four bodies.
> No sweet return for them,

> mother waiting, lilt
> of laughter at every corner. No,
> it's slink down back lanes,
> dodge their mocking eyes.
> Defeat bites deep.

Some have found the picture of the vanquished opponents cruel, but to Pindar's Greek sense of things it would have seemed the most natural way to convey the ecstasy of the victor, even if this poem had not required him to couple victory and defeat in the most emphatic way possible. In Greek you best describe A by setting it up against Z. A Homeric hymnist, wishing to paint the privileged joy of the immortals, does so by telling of the sorrowful condition of humanity, hopelessly subject to old age and death (*Hymn to Apollo,* 189 ff.).

From today's victor, a particular man, Aristomenes of Aigina, we move to man, universal man, at the pitch of fortune:

> Who wins some new fine thing,
> for the glory of it he flies
> lifted, hope-winged
> at the crest of man's estate.
> Wealth—what is wealth to this?

He rises, rises till he seems to fly, winged by hope that raises him above the normally granted reach. (Even at this point, the conventions of the genre are not forgotten, for "hope" is here the hope for a greater victory to come, and is followed, as we expect, by a warning of the fragility of good fortune.) Universalized still further, man in his joy becomes joy itself, joy that, by a process we accept because it is seen to be part of the rhythm governing all organic life on earth, brings with it its dark reverse:

Mortal delight
shoots up so fast and falls as quick to ground,
shattered by averse dispose.

The last two words are deliberately enigmatic in the Greek
and I have tried to leave them inscrutable. And now, embracing the entire human condition, the diapason from zero to all
imaginable overplus, comes the statement. The lines, the
greatest perhaps in Greek, have defeated all attempts at English translation and must be left in the original:

ἐπάμεροι· τί δέ τις; τί δ᾽ οὔ τις; σκιᾶς ὄναρ
ἄνθρωπος. ἀλλ᾽ ὅταν αἴγλα διόσδοτος ἔλθῃ,
λαμπρὸν φέγγος ἔπεστιν ἀνδρῶν καὶ μείλιχος αἰών.

(The bald prose of it: "Creatures of a day. What is he, what
is he not? Dream of a shadow, man. But when the radiance
granted by Zeus comes, a bright light rests on men and life
is sweet.") Only one translator meets the challenge, Hölderlin:

Tagwesen. Was aber ist einer? was aber ist einer nicht?
Der Schatten Traum, sind Menschen. Aber wenn der
    Glanz,
Der gottgegebene, kommt,
Leuchtend Licht ist bei den Männern
Und liebliches Leben.

A comparable passage of our own poetry may help us to
sound something of what is said in Pindar's Greek:

Men must endure
Their going hence even as their coming hither:
Ripeness is all.

Ripeness: the time for fruit to fall from the branch.

The ode ends with the poet bidding what we may take
to be his farewell to the island community he had served for
almost half a century. The lines, a solemn roll call of the great
names celebrated so often in the odes, are addressed to
Aigina, ancestral heroine and bride of Zeus:

> Mother, beloved, bring this city safely
> home on freedom's voyage. In the name of Zeus,
> Lord Aíakos, Peleus, brave Télamon, Achilles.

○ ○ ○

The achievement of Pindaric criticism in the last two decades has been to clear the odes of the extraneous historical
and biographical matter that had been read into them. The
danger is that critics may now be reading *out* of the odes a
good deal that is really there and in the process impoverishing
rather than purifying them. Pindar's task, as a victory poet,
we can all agree, was to praise the victor whose commission
(and money) he had accepted, and to do so in terms of the
epinician convention, a traditional form he had inherited and
must surely have greatly extended. We can agree too that a
poem of this sort, a public poem sung and danced by a chorus
of citizens, was no place to air his private interests and vex-
ations. Somewhere along the line, however, the question
comes: how much has to be excluded as irrelevant to the
poet's encomiastic task? He must not intrude his personal
affairs; are his deepest feelings about life also banned? And
what about matters which, while they may have no immediate
or obvious bearing on the victory that is being celebrated, may
be of active concern to the victor and his community? The
victor was after all a citizen, bound up with the life of his city

to a degree we can scarcely picture, and it is surely quite unhistorical to suppose that he thought of his achievement in isolation from that all-embracing life. To imagine him saying, whenever an ode seemed to treat of something other than his victory, "This is all very fine but what does it have to do with me?" is to attribute to a fifth-century Greek an individualism that belongs to an altogether later period.

Nonetheless, we all know the damage that can be done to a poem when alien circumstance is allowed to invade its territory, and the temptation to keep it out is strong. Pythian 8 is so fine a poem on a purely epinician reading that one is bound to feel reluctant to disturb its harmonies by exposing it to the discords of the public world. Our desire to protect the poem in this way, while it no doubt does us credit, is however distinctly a modern preference or prejudice, dating back hardly more than a century. Derived from the Symbolist movement with its doctrine of the purity of the poetic utterance and the call to exclude from a poem whatever is not poetry, it is appropriate only to work written within that tradition. We would be properly skeptical if a critic told us that a sonnet of Mallarmé could be understood only in the light of an episode from the Franco–Prussian war. Pindar, however, was not a Symbolist and held no doctrine of the purity of the poetic utterance, and if we are to exclude the public, political world from the odes it must be for different reasons, namely that like other Greek poets of the classical period his eyes went beyond the ephemeral to the permanent conditions of human life. It is only in that perspective and against that background that contemporary affairs are likely to enter into his work. Pythian 8 is indeed very much concerned with what is permanent in our condition, and if the poem is greater than we have yet seen, it is because it includes the issues of the day and by showing them to be subject to the universal laws

of existence makes them in some measure understandable
and hence bearable.

There is no question about the issue that must have been
uppermost in the minds of Pindar's Aiginetan audience when
Pythian 8 was performed there in 446. The situation, very
briefly, was this: in 458 the Peloponnesians together with their
Aiginetan allies fought a naval battle against the Athenians in
the waters off Aigina. The Athenians were victorious, landed
a force on the island and blockaded the town. The Aiginetans
resisted but were forced either the next year or the year after
to capitulate, upon which their walls were pulled down, their
fleet handed over to the victor, and they were reduced to the
humiliating status of a tribute-paying member of the Athenian
empire. In the decade that followed, Aigina saw her old maritime rival and adversary extend her activities over much of
the Mediterranean. To check the advance of Athenian power
on the Greek mainland, Sparta brought Thebes and other
Boiotian cities into a defensive alliance. Athens attacked and
by her victory at Oinophyta won control of the province except for Thebes. Ten years later—this brings us to the eve of
the performance of Pythian 8—the Athenians were defeated
at Koroneia and in the following year signed a thirty-year
peace with Sparta, surrendering some of the territory they had
acquired. Aigina, however, while regaining a measure of au-
tonomy, remained an Athenian tributary, her old proud in-
dependence gone. Now, no one can doubt that these events
must have been of the closest concern to Aiginetans. The
question is, what place, if any, do they have in a victory ode?

In his study of the Pythians, R. W. B. Burton remarks of
this poem, the invocation to Hesukhia, and her defeat of the
giants: "It may be unwise to read into this prelude too much
contemporary history and see Athens herself in Porphyrion
and Typho, but the company of Aiginetans who heard the

poem might well be compelled by their situation to make such a comparison" (176). Burton's book was published in 1962, the year which saw the appearance of Bundy's *Studia Pindarica*, hence before their lesson had been absorbed. Even so, his suggestion is made very cautiously and it does not quite face the critical issue. At issue is not whether the Aiginetans might have made such a comparison but whether Pindar intended them to do so. He would surely not have let the comparison arise unless he wanted them to find a reflection of their political situation in the poem. We should not of course look for any immediately topical reference—seeing in the defeat of the giants the Athenian defeat at Koroneia, for example. Current affairs do not intrude so bluntly into high lyric poetry. Nor is there any question of allegory, with Porphyrion and Typhon "standing for" imperial Athens. Allegory of that kind is not found in classical Greek poetry, and anyway Pindar is not writing allegory here but myth, something far more powerful. What we might expect, given Hesukhia's kinship with the divine beings married by Zeus when he set out on his *mission civilisatrice*, is that her conflict with the giants, reaching far beyond this or that military or political happening, points to the forces of cosmic disorder which constantly threaten the fragile order of things. We might expect, too, that in the poet's mind such events on the cosmic level have their correspondence on the earthly level. A theme of this sort can be very much at home in high poetry; we find it, for instance, in the first Pythian and in Horace's *Descende caelo*. In his fine reading of the Roman ode, Eduard Fränkel showed how much it gains if it is seen in the light of Pindar's Greek ode, and the process can be reversed (*Horace* [Oxford, 1957], 273 ff.). Both these great poems state a universal law: upstart pride and violence must take a fall. And give it its local application: the forces threatening Hellas, and those threatening the Roman state, will not prevail. Despite its briefer compass, the prelude to Pythian 8 is likely to have the same application and shadow forth the aggressive action of imperial Athens which was disturbing whatever peace and concord the Hellenic states enjoyed.

It would be wrong to label this politics and see it as something adventitiously inserted into a victory poem because it was on the poet's mind or because it concerned (or flattered) his hosts. To Pindar's unified vision, the universal, the political, and the athletic were intimately related. Hesukhia, the principle violated by Porphyrion and Typhon on the cosmic plane and by Athens on the political, is sustained and affirmed on the political plane by Aigina's seemly, traditional rule of life and on the athletic plane by her young athlete's success in the ordered ceremony of the games. The second, political plane, it may be said, is less evidently there in the poem and indeed not necessarily there at all. But surely it is implicit throughout—implicit, only, because such is the poet's art that, while there is nothing in the poem that cannot be taken in purely epinician terms (even if some things in it seem to call for further explanation), everything is made to point beyond itself and apply to the political situation, too grievous either to be forgotten or to be allowed to break disruptively into the celebratory occasion. Aigina's political situation is there, not as something the poet's listeners might be compelled to think of but as something he himself intended, in the fall of the giants brought down by Hesukhia, the virtue which made Aigina great, and in the figure of Too-Sure-of-Himself who will get a tumble at her rough hands in time. For Time is the father of all things and best savior of the just, as Pindar says elsewhere, and today's victor may prove to be tomorrow's vanquished. Aristomenes' fall on the bodies of his opponents tells of Aiginetan victory. It shows, too, how victory can carry within it the motions of defeat, just as in the myth the victory of the Successors brought only sorrow to the victorious captain. This island city where Justice lives fell, the poem declares, and indeed Aigina has fallen, fallen politically and also, a fall that carries the promise of new life to come, fallen "not far from the Graces." All human joy, shooting up so fast, falls in the end, shattered, bafflingly, by "averse dispose," a fall that can nonetheless be borne because it is part of the universal rhythm of life. In the perspective which the poem creates, one that reaches beyond sorrow to some encompassing serenity, the fall of an ancient city at the aggressor's hands is as grave as the fall of the leaf, no more, no less, and as inevitable. Ripeness is all. And what is victory but the other face of defeat?

The greatest poem of Pindar's that has come down to us, Pythian 8 shows how generous a scope this seemingly limited form can have. Arising from an occasion that hardly survived Pindar's lifetime and is wholly unfamiliar to us, governed by conventions that for centuries remained misunderstood and scarcely suspected, the victory ode has seemed little more than a literary sport. Today we think we understand its formal procedures rather well. We need now to go on to learn that in the hands of a great poet a strict convention is not a principle of exclusion but rather the means whereby whole reaches of experience are submitted to the shaping pressure of a poem's design. If Pindar praised men and their communities in a way never done before or since—so that the odes stand for us as the supreme example of a mode of poetry too little represented in our several literatures, the mode of celebration—he did not do so by tying one hand behind his back and excluding much of what most deeply concerned him. His odes are superbly disciplined compositions. They are also, in Ben Jonson's fine phrase, "ramm'd with life."

SELECTED
BIBLIOGRAPHY

Most Pindaric criticism is addressed to the classical specialist and, inevitably, has little to offer the common reader. Hence the brevity of this bibliography. The best general account of Pindar's work is to be found in the introduction to Frank J. Nisetich's translation of the odes.

Criticism

Bundy, Elroy L. *Studia Pindarica I and II*. Berkeley, 1962. For a brief account of these two papers which opened up the modern approach to Pindar, see chapter 1 of the present work. Too technical and containing too much untranslated Greek to be much use to the nonclassical reader.

Burton, R. W. B. *Pindar's Pythian Odes*. Oxford, 1962. Appearing just before Bundy's palace revolution took effect, these sober, careful readings of the twelve Pythian odes, though addressed to the classical specialist or would-be specialist, offer much help to the persevering general reader.

Fränkel, Hermann. *Early Greek Poetry and Philosophy*. Trans. Moses Hadas and James Willis. New York and London, 1973. Approaching Pindar from an older, German perspective, Fränkel offers a more thoughtful poet than the virtuoso technician of current Anglo–American criticism.

Mullen, William. *Choreia: Pindar and Dance*. Princeton, 1982. A daring, careful attempt to recover the crucial lost dimension of the odes, their realization in space and time as danced poems. Though addressed to the classical scholar, Mullen's approach has much to offer the general reader. The fine sense of Pindar's poetry informing this book is also found in Mullen's paper "Pindar and Athens: A Reading in the Aeginetan Odes" (*Arion*, n.s. 1/3, 1973–74).

Young, David C. *Three Odes of Pindar*. Leiden, 1968. The best place to go to discover how post-Bundy academic criticism sees Pindar. The reading of Pythian 11 is particularly valuable. (The nonclassicist will need to arm himself with a translation of the odes since the Greek is not translated.) By the same author: "Pindaric Criticism." In *Pindaros und Bakchylides*, ed. W. M. Calder III and J. Stern.

Darmstadt, 1970. A thorough survey of this somewhat dispiriting field.

Translations

The most useful is the most recent, *Pindar's Victory Songs*, trans. Frank J. Nisetich (Baltimore and London, 1980). *The Odes of Pindar*, trans. Richmond Lattimore (Chicago, 1947), and in the Penguin Classics series, *The Odes of Pindar*, trans. C. M. Bowra (Baltimore, 1969), may also be consulted. In the Loeb Classical Library, *The Odes of Pindar*, trans. Sir John Sandys (London and Cambridge, Mass., 1915), provides accurate prose versions in stilted, old-fashioned English. Among the rather few attempts to find a modern manner for Pindar and offer a poem for a poem, the most successful to date is Janet Lembke's version of Pythian 5 (*Arion* n.s. 2/2, 1975). Freer but very stylish are some versions by David Wevill: Pythian 9 (*Arion* 8/1, Spring 1969), Pythian 3 (*Arion* 8/4, Winter 1969), Olympian 6 (*Arion* 9/4, Winter 1970), Nemean 3 (*Delos* 6, 1971). *Pindar: Selected Odes*, trans. Carl A. P. Ruck and William H. Matheson (Ann Arbor, 1968), contains versions of twenty-one odes, perhaps the oddest and most extravagant to appear since Cowley (but then most translations of Pindar are far too flat), accompanied by engagingly speculative essays in interpretation.

Commentaries

Readers with enough Greek to tackle Pindar in the original (some Greek, any Greek, remembered from the classroom or acquired for the purpose) will find much incidental critical help in two older commentators, Basil Gildersleeve and J. B. Bury (see Abbreviations). Gildersleeve had a superb feeling for Pindar and could say more in a pithy, idiosyncratic sentence than most critics say in a page. Bury, though led astray by outmoded nineteenth-century theories of interpretation and unduly given to intrusive, overingenious fantasies of his own, was a sensitive verbal critic and possessed a fine sense of poetry.

INDEX